Dog Stories

Gregory C. DiFranza

ISBN-10: 154285640X
ISBN-13: 978-1542856409

DEDICATION

The book is dedicated to the memory of Faith, an
Airedale that is chronicled in this book. She taught me so
much about aggression and where it comes from. She
became the dog that Arlene and Stewart wanted her to
be. And she also became one of our absolute favorites to
have in the pack.
Rest in peace, sweet girl.

CONTENTS

ACKNOWLEDGMENTS

First and foremost, I'd like to thank my wife, Lisa, for being a great partner Pack Leader. I'd also like to thank Elena Elm-Bird, owner of Salty Paws Healthy Pet Market for her dedication to dogs from supplying their food and nutrition to being a cheerleader for behavior management and a huge supporter of what I do.

Without the dogs that I have met, clients I have had the pleasure of working with, and the people who refer problems to me this adventure wouldn't be possible.

Koa is the reason I do what I do because if it weren't for him, this adventure would be much harder and much more complicated. I recognized early on that his demeanor and outlook on life as a dog is what everyone would like to have in their dog. He is a great pack partner.

Introduction

For many years, I have taught people, and for the most part, law enforcement officers. My classes were conducted worldwide there were thousands and thousands of students during that time. My doctorate degree in education revolved around teaching multifaceted skills in a format designed to have the student remember their skills without constantly having to practice these skills. Not because they shouldn't but because they neither have the time nor the ability to do that in addition to doing their jobs. These classes also included teaching tactical units who do not have the occasion to work with a regular police canine unit how to work alongside the dog. And not get bitten in the process.

That part of my business started to wane thanks in large part to terrorism threats in many of my overseas clients' back yards. I was already learning the finer points of instinct and dog psychology through our Rhodesian Ridgeback, Koa. Observing how he interacted and corrected behavior, and the results that he achieved, gave me the idea that this was still teaching humans because the dogs already know what to do. It's just that the humans *want* a certain behavior but don't know *how* to relay that information to their dog.

I both volunteered at the Humane Society in Jacksonville, FL and started keeping people's dogs while they were away. Almost everyone would say that their dog had a certain quirk in one respect or another that would limit their activities or their socializing.

I love a challenge so I would set out to change their perception both by helping their dogs understand that they had no human limits and then showing them through pictures and videos what their dogs were up to during that time with us. And it was successful.

The same challenge went for the shelter where I worked my way into being able to handle to more aggressive dogs. I would usually handle them because 1) they were not as easy to get outside their kennel, and 2) I didn't come into the walk with preconceived notions about what would happen. And this was also successful.

Before this, I would often walk Koa with a group of friends who all had dogs on the beach in the morning, We would often see owners walking dogs that were completely out of control even on a leash and marvel how those folks were never admonished by Animal Control. So my friend Dan and I started joking about a boot camp style of morning walk: we would sprint a short distance, drop and do push-ups, sprint again, drop and do sit-ups, etc. And the joke was that the dogs would go with us and we would call it Kamp K-9.

That never really came to fruition but I took the idea and named the canine instruction aspect Kamp K-9 Jax Bch. From there, I started going to clients' houses and doing seminars around the Southeastern U.S. to teach people how to relate to their dogs in a calmer and less frustrated way; in essence, to become a better pack leader.

Now I conduct hands-on classes in pack leadership and use that as an avenue to show people that they can have the dog they *want*, as soon as they become the leader that their dog *needs*. Human training for the dogs' sake. These classes and my one-on-one classes have been used by rescue groups throughout the state and by now over a thousand clients.

This book is dedicated to a dog that was the first extremely dog aggressive case I ever worked. Faith became our sweetheart and was such a pleasure once she understood that she didn't need to correct every dog she came across. Although her story is chronicled starting in Chapter 62, she was a problem for her adopters to the point where they were unsure about being able to keep her. Already at 9 years old, this would not have been a good end for Faith. Arlene and Stewart Pessolano wanted to give her every chance to succeed and thanks to their determination and consistent pack leadership, Faith became the dog they wanted. Faith stayed with me several times even after I had stopped boarding other dogs because she was always a welcome guest for both Koa and our cat, Shaka.

I hope that you can learn something from this book of blog posts from my website that will help you have a better and calmer relationship with the dogs in your life, and hopefully make you a calmer, more assertive, and best pack leader your dog could ever hope to have!

5 Steps to Being a Pack Leader

At the end of each year, humans begin thinking about (or finally act on) getting a dog. Some people have never had a dog; some haven't had one in their adult life; and others have experience but it was with a dog much older than what they wound up getting. And almost all might start saying, "I didn't know what I was getting into with this guy/girl." Here are 5 steps to help you become a better pack leader to your new – or old – dog.

1. *Have the Right Energy*

   People often get a dog out of an emotional void in their own lives, and this is exactly the WRONG reason to get a dog. It's also unfair to put that kind of responsibility on a canine, who doesn't relate to the world emotionally. Calm and assertive (confident and consistent) is what they need, and a new dog will test your abilities. If you get frustrated, they stop listening. If you get upset, they stop listening. If you yell or get angry, they stop listening. Anything other than calm leadership will not result in a happy house/human/dog. So be the pack leader.

2. *Create the Rules*

I often hear owners ask me, "Is this okay?" Unless you have gone off the rails, your rules are your rules. The dog's job is to follow your rules and your lead. If that changes in the next 5 minutes, the dog's job is to follow. But create rules, don't let the dog create those rules… it never ends happily. Enforce the rules.

3. *Be Consistent*

Dogs respond best to a ritual; a pattern of behavior that can be counted on so they know for themselves what is expected. Unlike a recent "dog training" video I've seen, the trainer didn't want the dog going out the door ahead of him. He made the dog wait and give eye contact, then opened the door for the dog to go out ahead of him. What's the message? I honestly don't know, and neither will the dog.

Changing the rules to suit your desire is one thing; enforcing the rules already in place is another. Once again, enforce the rules.

4. *Fulfill your Dog*

Fulfillment is defined as contentment, serenity, completion. Letting your dog run in a back yard to "drain their energy" is incomplete pack leadership. Ever been so physically tired that you needed to go to bed but you couldn't sleep because your mind was racing? That's your dog! As soon as they are physically recharged (which generally doesn't take that long in the young ones) their mind tells them to get up and get going. Without mental and psychological challenges our dogs start chewing, ripping things up, tearing around the house like a crazy dog, and trying to get out of the house (often labelled by the owners as separation anxiety). Your "Leadership Walk" should be fulfilling several things: bonding, rules enforcement, following direction, having fun and sniffing, and a reinforcement for the both of you that you are a pack and the pack does things a certain way – calmly, until it's time to run around.

5. *Feel, Don't Think*

Dogs are instinctual and not emotional. Humans are intellectual, emotional, and to a small degree instinctual. But we don't nurture that part of our existence; we REALLY nurture the emotional side (some more than others!) and THAT'S where we start to make excuses for our dogs' behavior. "Well, he's a rescue," "He was attacked as a puppy," "He's had a hard life and he was abused," or "He doesn't like people who are _____ (fill in the blank: white, black, male, female, wearing hats, wearing beards, small dogs, big dogs, etc.)," all of which indicate that the human is trying to think their way into a solution and love the dog's bad attitude out of existence. Giving affection in that state of mind reinforces and rewards that state of mind. Short answer? Don't do that! Be the role model for that behavior that you wish to see in your dog – if you wanted your child to stand a certain way you would probably say, "Stand like this," and then demonstrate that posture. State of mind is no different, but you are going to have to challenge yourself to be a better teacher for your dog.

I have also started a video blog on Facebook called "Dog Talk! With Pack Leader. Today's installment is exactly what we ended on here: making excuses for your dog's behavior, or your shortcomings as a leader. They're short, quick, to the point, and public so go to:

www.facebook.com/DogtalkwithPackLeader

My other pages are public as well; search for Greg DiFranza and or:

www.facebook.com/kampk9jaxbch.

Until the next time, have a joyous holiday season with your dog and I'll see you next year (well, 2 weeks, really)!

Aggression is Aggression, Regardless of the Breed

D uring the yearly visit to the vet with Koa, I watched as a vet tech carried a Chihuahua back to the owner who just finished telling me how antisocial the dog is to everyone and everything. The dog looked fine until being handed to the owner who said, "Here's the little trouble maker now," and held the dog high on his chest. The dog, who had previously been just fine, snapped at the vet tech's face – who was taken aback just a bit and since I had a front row seat I admit it was pretty close!

Look at the picture accompanying this chapter. Neither behavior is acceptable but small dogs seem to do this more often than the larger breeds, and are able to get away with this more often... do you know why this is? Because the small breeds are seen as "cute" and having "lots of personality", when the truth is that they are given a free ride by their owners and that behavior is never corrected effectively. In this case, the owner told her "No" while stroking her head and making excuses for the behavior. Can you imagine doing that with a Rhodesian Ridgeback or a German Shepherd who is aggressive and snapping at someone? Just stroke their head and nurture that behavior – and get out your checkbook because that is going to be a trip to the hospital for someone...

This dog was not "antisocial" as the owner had stated; the dog was the pack leader and the owner demonstrated weakness which causes the dog to go into leader mode to fill the void. How do I know this? While we sat in the waiting room before going with the vet tech, calm and balanced Koa was watching the dog from his usual respectful distance and the dog – while in its owner's lap – stared at Koa and shook. This isn't fear, but confusion about what to do and it is negative energy being thrown off (in short, this dog would be fine around other dogs WITHOUT the owner's negative energy being present). Being Unbalanced in the face of Balance creates confusion and anxiety, which are good things when it helps the dog to become more balanced. But nurturing that anxious/nervous behavior will lead to aggression and a possible bite – and the owner is not immune. Since the dog is the leader and does not respect the human's position in the pack, if they can't bite the object of their rage or fear they will bite the next best thing.

In fact, when you review the TIMING and ERGONOMIC DYNAMICS of the behaviors it is textbook dog psychology. So how can this be changed?

1. When holding a small dog, **hold them lower than your face/chest area.**
2. If the dog has a history of aggressive behavior **stop it BEFORE it shows itself.**
3. **Follow through on the corrections** and be calm and assertive setting **rules/boundaries/limitations** on behaviors.
4. **Don't make excuses for the behavior but do apologize.** First of all, your excuses are probably wrong. Second, people have far more patience with owners and the dogs that are aggressive if you tell the truth – that you are working to make your dog social. And last, when you get tired of apologizing for your dog you will cause the change to take place.
5. **Be Patient!** Frustration is weakness so take a breath.

6. **Make your dog social.** Staying calm, expecting the desired result, and exposing your pack member to as many different environments as possible – and often – creates the trust and respect they should see in you, and the ability for them to associate calm appropriate behavior with new people/dogs/experiences. Take them to a dog park, to the pet store, to the hardware store (many stores allow dogs on leashes), around crowds (Rita's and Bruster's have free doggie ice cream for them and it's a good excuse for you to reward yourself!), or anywhere that you think would be a challenge for you or your dog.

7. Remember **exercise, discipline, affection** –in that order!

Until next time remember, no excuses for your dog – or for you!

Draining Excess Energy

There are quite a few people who don't believe they have the time to walk their dogs to drain the energy – and you may be right! "The Walk" is really not designed for physical energy draining since it is really all about the mental challenge. However, if you have a treadmill (and many people do) you already have one tool available; the other tool is patience.

It is true that some treadmill bands are too short for some dogs (Koa is an example) and that is not the norm. But a patient attitude and a calm demeanor is really important, and you would be surprised how quickly your dog will learn to walk on it! Plus, behavior issues are easier to control and to correct without the pent up anxious energy that they may have.

Kobe and Remy (pictured and in Chapter 40) had never been on a treadmill before their vacation with me when their owners were out of town. Both did not get all of their energy out earlier in the day and they both really needed a run. I had rollerbladed with them several days before but they needed something a bit cooler so I decided to try the treadmill. As you can see it works really well and although you'll need to stay there with them in the beginning, they get a great walk and a mental challenge all at once. Each time after the first time it was easier and easier for them to recognize what they would be doing and they certainly looked happy.

Even though your dog might protest in the beginning, setting the correct pace and helping them adjust is a good mental exercise for the Pack Leader, also. And it gives them one more reason to respect your position in the pack with the challenge and the correct mental attitude.

Try it and let me know how it worked for you. If it didn't work, let me know and I can help with the exercise. Until next time, stay calm and get your energetic pup exhausted!

How to Create Calm

W elcome to the new year! Let's start this year by going back to basics: calm energy for you and your dog. Many times, people inadvertently create the problems that cause people to need "training for their dogs". The reality is that the training needs to take place for the humans and while many of my clients do realize this in advance, they don't truly understand that the dog can change rather quickly when its environment – meaning the human equation – changes. But how do you achieve that "calm" state of mind?

Calm is the foundational aspect of true leadership. Many people have extremely stressful jobs and they are phenomenal in that job as leaders yet somehow that doesn't translate when they return home to their furry family. I believe that it's also a human need to not be totally committed to leadership ALL of the time, especially when we are in our "relaxation place". Our dogs provide unconditional love, at least as we sometimes view their behavior, and we can just sit back and bathe in the glory of dogs.

But they NEED what we MUST provide to them: structured lives, controlled state of mind, living in the moment instead of living in the past, and both mental and physical challenges to nurture their animal/dog/breed requirement. Without this, dogs will view their pack as weak and requiring leadership. Just like humans, when being thrust into a position and environment or job that is uncomfortable or beyond the ability of the person, dogs will also begin to exhibit behaviors which are anti-social and virtually unproductive for the rest of the pack. Those behaviors will be nervous or anxious, too much energy all the way to the other end of the spectrum at aggression, resource guarding, and biting or snapping at humans including the owner.

It is at this point where humans begin to sense that they are not in control and frankly they are wrong: they actually lost control WAY before they begin to realize it because they make excuses and anthropomorphize (humanize) their dogs by putting human emotions into what they

THINK their dog(s) are thinking. Once again, this is weakness in the canine world and creates more of an uncomfortable environment for the dog. And the cycle continues.

You love your dog... but do you love your dog in the way that THEY need to be loved? If you are not providing calm leadership, you are not loving your dog the best way that you can. Being calm is easy when things are going right but how do you stay calm when things are going wrong?

1. Take a "combat breath": in for a 4 count, hold it for a second, let it all out. Clear your mind, move forward.
2. Think of a leader that you admire and model their outlook and behavior pattern (don't imitate, use it as a MODEL for your behavior).
3. A dog's reality is their senses: ENERGY, nose, eyes, ears. That's it. Have that become YOUR reality, not just emotional, intellectual or spiritual.
4. Concentrate on the positives for you AND the dog. I once had a client who told me their dog was a 30%'er one day. I asked what happened and they said that he had gotten excited at the sight of another dog and that they had corrected it and

everything was fine afterwards. I remarked that I would have said 95% at the lowest and probably higher. Don't concentrate on the negatives.

5. Take time for you, and enjoy the time you do have with your dog. There ARE people who would love to have a dog but can't for one reason or another. Remember this when you are with your dog.

6. Challenge yourself as well as the dog. The more often you and the dog complete a challenge together as a team, the tighter a bond you will have with your dog. Go places you haven't gone before, do things you haven't done. When they were renourishing the beaches years ago, Koa and I would jump onto the large pipe that extended out into the ocean from the sand and Koa would not only hurdle it, but he would also "tightrope it" all the way to the water and back.

7. Spend time in nature. Beaches, rivers, waterfalls, mountains, trails, fields: all are within a few miles of wherever you are reading this. Go, clear your mind, breath, experience where you are. Pause to reflect on nothing and the more you do this the better you will get at it, perhaps to the point where you can do this even while overseeing and managing your environment. When you do this, you are being calm & assertive!

Until the next time, be a calm, assertive, and positive role model for someone else!

Is A "Trained Dog" A "Calm Dog"?

I often hear from clients that their dog has gone through a variety of classes at different locations: pet shops, trainers' businesses, etc. And they either passed or they were "kicked out" because of a host of reasons. Mostly, the dog trainer was not well-versed or comfortable (or it wasn't in the curriculum) to deal with a dog that was not "perfect".

And they call because the dog in their pack is not doing the things they want them to do; namely, be better behaved or stop biting at people and/or dogs, and to stop pulling on the leash and making walks so uncomfortable and stressful that they just stop walking the dog.

I'm sure you've heard or read from me that a lot of those behaviors are an outgrowth of two things: lack of appropriate leadership and too much energy. I've written about leadership (and will again in the future) but I wanted to share with you an analogy that I use and make it visual. If we don't assist our packs with draining some of the pent-up energy they have, our dogs will act out in ways that are unproductive: chewing, picking up everything, food stealing (counter surfing), horrible leash and walk manners, etc. And we also want it fixed NOW, which – by the way – is not the way it happens. There is no time schedule for working with your dog, you just have to stay consistent. Become your dog's personal trainer for mind and body!

So I want you to look at the series of pictures that I made to portray this. These are to portray the water (energy) in the glass (our dogs) and where the levels need to be for things to be 1) better managed, or 2) more helpful for the dog's mental and physical health.

The first one is where your dogs' energy level needs to be before leaving for the day, or at the end of the evening, or before we plan to have guests visit, because it will take a while for their energy level to get to a less manageable level.

This second one is usually where we leave our dogs' energy level. It's not hard to figure out how soon the energy level will fill and start to overflow. Overflowing is where we start to see and experience the "bad behaviors".

This third one shows what happens when, while you're gone the phone rings, the mail people come, the UPS delivery takes place, someone rings the doorbell, etc. Energy levels and excitement increase dramatically!

This fourth one shows where, depending upon how little

space is left, the next event starts to really become a problem.

The last ones show how when the energy becomes too much for the dog to take and it starts to flow freely out of the dog. Eating blinds, chewing holes through walls, WAY too much excitement when you get back home, are all symptoms of this overflowing energy.

Your leadership walk needs to take place and probably a bike ride, rollerblade, skateboard activity (NOT you running the dog – unless it's a small dog, you are probably tired by the end but your medium to large breed can go much further/faster/longer than you) to help regain the calmer state of mind in your dog. So remember to help your dogs' state of mind by helping drain the energy, staying calm, and staying consistent.

Until next time, stay calm and be your dog's personal trainer!

BEWARE!!!

B runo, Ginger, Bogle, Rooney, Parker, Bella (2), Paisley, Mollie, Emily, Banana, Alfred, River, Zeus, Kacey, Nemo, Daisy, Harpo, Dixie, Cosmo, Stella (2), Hershey, Baxter, Ella, Dallas, Molly, Patton, Ryder, Luke (2), Suze, Millie. What do these dogs and their Pack Leaders have in common? Since a seminar I did in February 2015, I've had the distinct pleasure and honor to work with all of them on behavioral issues. And these didn't include our guys and gals who are taking the hands-on classes, or the ones on the schedule that I haven't gotten to work with, yet!

The owners also all have something else in common: an unending love for their dog with behaviors that their pack leader would like to see different, and (for the most part) a commitment by their pack leader to stay consistent with the ritual of leadership. But if they don't, or if all of the pack leaders in the house are not on the same page, the dog will not progress and their stressful lives (humans and animals) will NOT change. In fact, oftentimes, it gets worse because in the dog world it is a weak environment. But even children can become a pack leader; it happens with my clients all of the time!

Another thing the dogs have in common is that they all have too much energy without the right kind of leadership, and that always spells trouble and frustration. WALK YOUR DOG, and stay in control of yourself AND them. The Walk is psychological exercise and by its nature is not physically draining; although the owners have seen their dogs lay down to take a nap immediately following my walk with them.

Calm state of mind in the dog equals less or no behavior issues. Dogs are ritualistic so staying consistent is a key element of rehabilitation. Then, the humans can have the life they envisioned with their dog by their side. Some of the success stories are: going out to eat in public at a sidewalk café for the first time – ever; having an entire neighborhood be able to come together outside with their dogs calm and mostly off-leash around each other; calmly walking or running alongside of them without the pulling and wrestling match on the leash; stopping the bad behavior of rushing the door and jumping on visitors; having their dogs be calm and social with new dogs after severe aggression before kept them from having conversations. And the list goes on.

Why and how can this happen in a two-hour session? Because I treat the dogs with respect as a dog and then teach the owners how to emulate that behavior. The dogs ALWAYS understand and follow the program rather quickly, even the aggressive ones. In fact, especially the aggressive ones. BEWARE of "training programs" that claim to take your dog away for a couple of weeks for thousands of dollars and return to you a "trained dog" because the dog is returning to the same unbalanced way the owner has treated them. Some of my clients are ex-clients of these folks. Beware of "dog trainers" who will sell you an e-collar for 4-5 times the price to accomplish "obedience". Some of my clients are ex-clients of these folks. Beware of programs that claim to "speak to the dog" by taking your hard-earned money teaching you how to "grab the dog's face and bark into it (yes, this is real, and they do NOT offer reconstructive surgery after you get your face bitten!) Some of my clients are ex-clients of these folks. And beware of training programs that promise you obedience training which is treat-based only as a "one size fits all" category of taking your money. Sadly, a lot of my clients have had these experiences and then contact me because all the other methods are not working.

They don't work because they are not based in dog psychology and a mutual respect of the animal/dog/breed and creating leadership not "alphas" – they are based on human psychology applied to dogs. They represent a valiant and successful effort to steal your money and not help the dog, or you in the long run. The reason for unwanted behavior falls into major categories (too much energy, selecting a dog that does not match your family's energy level or other dynamics within the family – domestic unrest or still grieving over humans or dogs who have passed) but you cannot treat each symptom of unwanted behavior by itself. You treat the cause of the behavior, then you correct as necessary. For how long? For the life of the dog; but once they understand the rules (and they do), you will correct much less frequently than when they are new, or puppies.

Until the next time, walk your dog (if your dog is too fat (or misbehaves) then you are not getting enough exercise!) and keep being your dog's calm leader!

Leadership

What in the world is a cat doing in a dog book? Well, this is Shaka, and he is a 3-year old Blue Point Birman who is always at the house and is ALWAYS off limits to every dog that comes into the pack. The reason Shaka is gracing the front of this chapter is because of his leadership with dogs. He corrects with calm/assertive energy. He's not mean to them; he is assertive, which is what every dog is also looking for in a pack leader aside from being calm.

This is not to say that Shaka always knew what to do around the dogs. In fact, he had to learn that running is a game and creates excitement in the dogs; therefore, they chase. However, when he stops he gives the Pack Leader look that says, "Knock it off!" He also has learned that if a dog is too intense and too curious that I'll make the corrections (I'm a cat pack leader, too? A pack is a pack...)

but if I'm too far away he can correct on his own. Rarely does this mean that he swats them away. Sometimes just his own "Tsch!" sound changes their state of mind, but sometimes they are too close and he "touches" to snap them out of their thought process.

Only once have I seen him actually pursue one of the dogs, but he did it to Stella because she was not in the right state of mind when she walked away and so Shaka had to "follow through" with the message being sent. Therefore, Shaka puts into practice all of the techniques that I talk about with changing a dog's behavior.

Recently I've had Luci (Great Dane/Lab mix) at Kamp K-9 Jax Bch. Luci has not had a problem with Shaka but really chases the cats in her neighborhood or the ones that stray into her yard. Shaka has gotten very good at judging a dog's energy and possibilities and he never had a problem with Luci. I think this confused Luci and she became curiously interested in this cat that doesn't run and isn't upset by her sniffing around him. In fact, Luci came up to Shaka the other day and started just barking at him, almost to say, "What are you doing just lying there in front of me?"

That's when it dawned on us what Shaka has really been doing with the dogs all this time. Shaka laid on the floor and looked PAST Luci and ignored her, slowly flicking his tail and no matter how loud she got he ignored her and never flinched. And she walked away and laid down very resigned and calm/submissive.

There are those who write reams and talk incessantly about how this type of dog behavior training is wrong; that you should use treats, and spend thousands of dollars "training" your dog, never correct them, never enforce rules/boundaries/limitations, instinct training is all tricks, etc. And yet, here is an entirely different species who has never been to "dog behavior instructor training", doesn't have any certifications, is sometimes known as a sworn enemy of canines (and vice versa), has never watched TV or the Dog Whisperer and he knows INSTINCTUALLY what to do to change a dog's state of mind. Calm/assertive energy, send the right message, touch correct to change the state of mind if sound didn't work or when the dog is not giving respectful space to another pack member, follow through on the message you are sending, no touch/no talk/no eye contact with a dog that has the wrong energy until they calm down, and know when to address behaviors and when to ignore them.

Until the next time, stay calm & assertive with ALL of the species in your pack!

Energy & Leadership

These are two of the biggest deficiencies that dog owners have: their dog has too much energy (and they don't know what to do about it) and there is a breakdown in leadership in the dog's mind.

If your dog has too much energy it will be much more difficult to have the dog pay attention to your direction. It's not a matter of physical energy as much as it is mental energy; because of this, simply throwing a ball or a Frisbee over and over and over again does not challenge your dog mentally and therefore they can do that forever and ever without getting "tired". Learn to bike with your dog (there are inexpensive 3 wheel versions available if you are afraid of being pulling down), rollerblade, or challenge them mentally in waiting until the ball is thrown again. The point is always to put your dog in a calm state of mind before an activity begins so that the association is calm/submissive state before rewards are given.

Human Leadership is the other deficiency. Allowing your dog to go out of doors first, into dog parks first, pulling you around on the walk, deciding when they will get on furniture/beds/car seats, etc., are all deficiencies in leadership. Just because you are the leader of the free world, as in the accompanying photos, doesn't mean you can lead in the animal/dog world. And please don't think I'm only selecting one president – I have similar photos spanning all the way back to Kennedy.

Leadership is being confident in your abilities and demonstrating this in a calm state of mind no matter what is stressing you out. In a recent dog class I conducted, I had everyone in the class walk a particularly high energy canine student by themselves. The point was to demonstrate leadership in a dog that is not yours just by taking the leash. It caught some pack leaders off-guard because they were focused on their dog which is a different and lower energy, but all discovered that once you set and enforce rules in a calm state the dog can and does respond immediately.

Until the next time, stay calm/assertive and be a real leader for your dog!

Staying Consistent with your Training

A question that I'm often asked is, "How soon should I start working with my dog?" Here's a blueprint!

When Do We Start?

These pictures are from Koa's first full day with us at 10 weeks old. Starting your work with your dog doesn't have

to be at this age, but the sooner the better. Why? Because they need to learn that you're the one in charge and in control of how they spend their time on the walk. Remember that this can take place at any age since it is all about you and your energy. Staying calm, learning to come, and learning to walk on a loose leash are skills you and your dog will need for the rest of your time together. Does this mean they don't get a chance to be a dog?

Supplement Your Work with Play

Of course not! Playtime is affection, and once the exercise & discipline part of the walk has been accomplished it's time for everyone (including you) to play and have fun – to bond with your dog. This is also affection, but affection can also be as transparent as enjoying the walk itself. They

don't need treats, they don't need petting, but these are powerful tools when used at the correct time. After play time, it's time to go back to work so that the ritual remains the same and the dog can be comfortable in his/her expectation. And then end your walk on a calm, positive note!

As Pack Leader, YOU Dictate the Time for Everything

Rules, boundaries, limitations, and protection and direction. These are what we true Pack Leaders offer our pack, in a calm and balanced way. Yes, even when our packs do something that "embarrasses" us. Change your perception: Be embarrassed if you don't make corrections or walk in a calm but assertive fashion. You know that when you watch another dog handler being too rough, frustrated and angry, that person is not a role model for you. At least I hope not!

Be the Role Model

Be the role model for other handlers, and be the role model for your dog through your energy. We also have the power to change other people through our actions and

demeanor. When someone watches you, and says, "I want my dog to be like that!" it starts with your ability to be a confident Pack Leader and put in the work. There is no easy button, no magical transformation. Different handlers get different responses, correct? That is due to the different energies.

Until next time, take your dog for a walk and enjoy your time together!

Visualize What You Want!

"You are what you eat," suggests that we are only as good as what we put into our bodies. The same goes for what is in our minds at any given time. In the dog world it's known as energy – in the human world, mind-set. Either way you term it, your dog knows how you feel. In this chapter we are just going to concentrate on seeing success.

In my tactical police courses, I teach extensively about the survival mind-set and how what is called "feed forward" sometimes can dictate life or death for the officer. In judo matches at the world championship level I have to see myself being successful or I most certainly will not be – and it's resulted in seven world judo championships. Any highly successful person sees themselves winning before they even begin – not arrogantly, but confidently and humbly, and they see all the steps in winning being performed perfectly in their heads long before the competition be it sports, business, or personal.

SEEING yourself winning is as important as having the skills to survive – at times even more so. But while we can bluff our way past a human encounter, you can't do that with a dog. Why? Can they read our minds? Well, no... and yes!

In the photo accompanying this chapter, I'm walking three powerful large breeds with a loose leash (two Rhodesian Ridgebacks and a Blue Bay Shepherd). No one is pulling, lunging, playing wrestling games. Do they at some point? Sure, but are they directed properly? Again, sure they are. That's my job as a pack leader – not to keep them from having fun, but I have the responsibility of keeping them SAFE. This was taken right after a jog in the ocean with all three, and it was a wild and extremely fun time. Walking calmly afterwards is also wild and extremely fun!

And the best part? YOU can do the same thing, IF you see it happening in your mind. If you see three out-of-control warrior dogs dragging your carcass down the beach face first (like in a movie), then THAT is very likely to happen! See yourself in control, walking and enjoying the beach and the sunshine, and helping these dogs be better at being dogs (and perhaps even a role model for others) then THAT is what the dogs – and other humans – will see.

Until next time, enjoy the leadership position and see yourself winning!

Human Behavior vs. Dog Behavior

Part of my tactical presentations to police and military personnel worldwide is the exploration of human behavior responses and recognizing the motivation behind the behavior to devise a better and more effective response in return.

One aspect that follows closely in the dog world is called, "Psycho-Physiological Response to Threat Stress" which most of us only know as "Fight or Flight". Those are only two of four possible responses to threat stress – the other two are Posturing (or Avoidance) and Acceptance (or Submission).

Humans and dogs are both part of the Animal Kingdom, so our responses will be very similar with one major difference and this difference can have either a fatal outcome or a successful one. The difference is in how we read the behaviors. Since we are talking about dogs, we'll keep it simple.

Dogs react to a perceived threat in a certain order and it almost always follows this order: Fight or Flight, Avoidance, Submission. Humans, not so much. Humans can get stuck in one response over and over until it proves fatal to them (or the other combatant). However, since dogs are really motivated by balance they do strive to get balanced but they first have to drain the anxious energy that they are experiencing. Anxiety without a release leads to dominance, and dominance can lead to aggression.

When we are able to get our dogs' state of mind to the avoidance stage (avoidance, not flight) then we are much closer to the submissive stage, which is where the dog finds peace and balance. Strong, calm and assertive pack leaders leading the dog into this area of thought are necessary to achieve this state of mind. As pack leaders, we should remember that the dog is a mirror into our own behaviors and state of mind: if we are nervous, the dog will be anxious. If we are fearful, the dog will be dominant. Any state of mind other than calm/assertive is a sign of weakness and in the primal dog world, weakness is dealt with by expelling the weak state or killing it. In the domestic dog world, they believe that they must take on the leadership role because to them there is no one there to be the leader so it must be them! That is where you find aggression, which causes confusion and tension and is much more difficult to regain without a strong pack leader.

That is why it is easier to regain leadership status when we can remove the source of weakness. Many times, this means removing the owners temporarily to be able to put the dog back into the follower mode. The pack leader needs to be patient and calmer than the dog is aggressive and if you want to be a strong pack leader, you must become an expert at reading dog body language because this will tell you what state of mind the dog has.

Want to know the biggest problem with humans? They misread a dog's body language and assign it human meaning then they act according to this misinformation. Which can get you or someone else seriously hurt ("The dog is happy – see how he wags his tail?" Aggressive dogs – police canines, for example – wag their tails the entire time they're ripping a suspect to shreds, because it is exciting to them and you may even see sexual excitement in that same dog. That does not mean he wants to date the suspect!).

Remember to learn to read a dog, and if you're not sure ask someone who truly knows! Or, stay tuned to this book where we'll be exploring that subject!

Reading Canine Body Language:
Part 1

In the human world, 93% of all communication is non-verbal, which means body language and vocal inflection. People listen and respond to only 7% of what is ACTUALLY said. In the animal world, it is slightly different in that there are no dialects; there is only energy and body language. Body language and the communication meanings behind the sounds that are made are extremely important. You cannot put one meaning above the other without taking all of it into context, just as humans cannot accurately receive a message without all of the parts being considered.

There is something to be said about how simply dogs interact with each other; it is another about how humans interact with EVERYTHING around them and make it complicated. This is Part 1 of a two-part series on what

Canine Body Language is, not as we humans wish to believe it to be.

Recently I was walking Koa in Home Depot and talking about dogs with one of their associates when a couple walked up and asked, "Does he bite?" Of course, the very truthful answer is that ALL dogs bite, it's all about WHEN not IF. As I started to smile before I could answer that he does not, the associate handled it for me by answering, "Do you think he'd have a dog that big in here if he DID bite?"

I appreciate people asking if they can pet Koa before they do (although I don't require that) because they should know if a dog is a problem if they do not know the dog. However, I trust Koa 110% around everyone – people, children, dogs – because we have, and still do, put in the work to make that a reality. When a dog barks or wags its tail is it aggressive? Happy? Anxious? Unsure? Warning you about an outside danger? Inviting another dog to play? Or communicating to another dog to quit goofing around?

Sometimes we can tell by the pitch and volume what message a human is trying to send; dogs are no different. However, humans put human emotions in the meaning of what animals do. When a dog wags their tail, does that mean they are not a threat and mean you no harm, or do you just wish that is the reason they're staring at you and wagging their tail because you REALLY want to pet that dog? (By the way, the answer is he/she could absolutely be a threat – it has to be taken into context.)

Please remember that all behaviors can quickly change and that sometimes one behavior leads to another, which is why it is important to stop unwanted behaviors BEFORE they get out of control. However, to do that, we have to know what we are looking at. Ultimately, we want our dogs to have a measure of self-control so that we can monitor but not have to control their behaviors 100% of the time with people and other dogs.

As you can see from the graphic accompanying this chapter, a few behaviors pull at our heartstrings – anxious/nervous, and frightened. The WORST thing you can do with dogs exhibiting these behaviors is to give affection ("It's okay, Barfy, don't be scared."). The dog sees this as acceptance of this behavior when they are really saying that they are unsure and need leadership. If it doesn't come their way they will react out of indecision; this usually means trying to pet the dog when it is not the right time, or thinking that the dog is being stubborn and "acting like a baby" (yes, I have read and seen this with my own eyes!). Which is a great way to get bitten, and then we mislabel the dog "aggressive" when it was humans who were ignorant and disrespectful of the dog's confusion.

Another misunderstood behavior is alert (mistaken for interested) and dominance (misread by thinking they are playful). We may see these behaviors as one activity when in reality it is many activities rolled into one. Interested is fine but it can go to dominant or aggressive very quickly, so this attitude has to be monitored and controlled.

Probably the most misunderstood body language is the difference between playful and aggressive. Because dogs do not use English for their verbal language skills, many people hear dogs barking and moving quickly as aggression, and vice versa (not recognizing aggression and believing that the dog is playing). So what is the difference? Aggression is a more targeted stance and body movement, where being playful or inviting another dog to play is bouncier and more carefree – and not targeted. A dog that barks and runs along a fence with another dog can be playing and inviting play. It is aggression when the dog cannot leave that behavior, begins barking in a very one-dimensional way, and charges at in an attempt to go through the fence. Being territorial does not mean aggressive; territorial is, "This is my place," and aggressive is, "You are not a threat but I'd kill you if this fence wasn't here."

All domestic dogs were bred from wolves to be guards, security from physical threats, and hunters; companionship came with the rest of those jobs. If your dog is too territorial and aggressive they need more exercise (and do not say, "But I have a BIG backyard," because that is not a challenge to them) and more boundaries BEFORE they exhibit the unwanted behaviors. In other words, they need a job. Respect the Animal, Dog, Breed in your companion so that they can be Name last. Unless you've named them Trouble, in which case this makes my point about humans…

Part 2 will discuss how to practice corrections in a way that won't take all day and will create the type of relationship you want your dog to have with the outside world. Until then, become a reader – of Canine Body Language!

Reading Canine Body Language: Part 2

In Part 1 we examined what you are actually looking at when you see your dog, or another dog, assuming a certain stance. Now let's look at how and when to limit the behavior that triggers a response that you don't want to deal with.

Everyone who has owned a dog knows that dogs want to see and meet other dogs. However, how do we do this without the lunging and pulling that goes along with that type of meeting? First, your dog needs to be in a calm state before the nose-to-nose type of meeting, otherwise it could trigger a fight. Secondly, YOU control the meeting and the time spent (rules/boundaries/limitations). Just today, our Beach Pack met Dexter, a Great Dane/Rhodesian Ridgeback mix and huge guy who is only 2 years old. Obviously, everyone wanted to see everyone else, but it had to be on the Pack Leaders' terms. They all calmly approached nose-to-nose and butt to butt with no explosions of energy (usually a sign that someone is unbalanced even if it is only to play) and after the initial greetings stood calmly while we all talked about Dexter. Two Beach Patrol volunteers walked past and asked if they all knew each other and, of course, the answer is, "Now they do!" But I also added that this is what happens when a balanced pack meets a new dog who is also balanced; there is no pulling, no barking, no running around, no lunging. If there is, pack leaders need to walk their dog away from that because it can get out of hand very quickly. Most important was the fact that the pack is calm BEFORE the actual meeting – catch unwanted behavior before it gets uncontrollable.

Another element that the vast majority of dog owners do not understand is the myth that dogs should never meet face to face because that is a challenge to the other dog. In fact, wolves will smell the teeth of another wolf or of a human when first meeting (once they decide to get that close to you). If the dog (yours or the other) is exhibiting dominant behavior and posture, then the likelihood of it going bad is pretty high. The goal is calm/interested or curious behavior (not even submission, which could be viewed as weakness and able to be dominated). Remember that dogs are smell-oriented first, so they smell faces first ("What'd you have for breakfast?") and then move to the rear ends ("What's you have for dinner last night?") and it is all completely normal AND ABSOLUTELY NECESSARY THAT THE OWNER ALLOW THIS TO HAPPEN. Why? Because if you jerk your dog away or give a correction for normal dog behavior, the message sent is that you are trying to protect your dog from the other dog, and if there is truly nothing wrong (and usually there isn't) the dog may feel a need to defend itself and they are a lot closer to the "threat" than you are. So a fight breaks out… caused by you!

If you are unsure about meeting another dog your dog will be unsure (remember mirrored behavior!). Take them to dog parks, watch how they all interact, and enjoy the outside as your dog enjoys it! And stop being ultra-protective about every little move they make (do YOU like being micromanaged??). The more your dog realizes that you understand them, the calmer they will be, but only if YOU are a calm/assertive and knowledgeable Pack Leader! Until next time, raise your Canine Literacy Rate and keep reading – canine body language!

The Importance of Being the Leader
Your Group Needs

I n the Animal Kingdom, just as in the human business world, the very survival of the group depends upon the right kind of leadership, not just someone who is "in charge". Therefore, in the wild, leadership qualities are a matter of life and death; consider that in a wolf pack, sometimes consisting of 40-50 animals, if a leader becomes unbalanced and without calm, assertive leadership often the rest of the pack will kill that leader. This is because of simple, yet time honored operational success principals that the survival of the group is more important than the survival of one individual.

While that may seem harsh, we have to explore why that is so important in the wild: 1) no one knows when and where the next meal will be coming (or how big it will be), 2) whether they will be attacked for operating in another's territory, and 3) that the group's success lies in the reproduction within the pack to continue the pack's progress as well as its survival. While the correlation to the human business world is glaringly obvious, wolf packs can exist for decades in the harshest of environments while human businesses sometimes never even get off the ground, much less stay in business for very long. So what's the difference and what can we learn from our furry friends?

Humans are the only grouping within the Animal Kingdom who follow, and often times will elevate, an unbalanced individual to be in a leadership position. In canine behavioral training, I show owners how changing their leadership position within their "pack" will often instantly change the behavior of their dog, when the behavior ranges from too anxious, unsettled, anti-social, or aggressive towards everything and everyone. The vast majority of canines are followers, and that is their strength. They follow directions from leaders, they do the work to the best of their abilities, and they support the balanced leaders. They are also the individuals who will eliminate the unbalanced leader from their midst.

Canines also will fill a void that exists in leadership positions, often to an unproductive end. Followers who are thrust into leadership positions unwillingly will often "act out" because they are way out of their comfort zone and operating beyond their skill set. Dogs, being purely perceptual beings, can give us instant feedback as to how well we are doing in our leadership roles. Humans are intellectual/spiritual/emotional and that drives us differently – we think beyond the present and try to create strategies for our futures.

Another component of leadership is knowing how to follow. Often have we hear the grumbling after a company disaster and the conversation revolves around "horrible" and "stupid" decisions management made. While part of that may be true, even the best ideas without people to do the work to the best of their ability will guarantee failure. That is instability on the part of the workers/followers. If a leader has never been a follower, they will not understand how the strength of the group is in their unity. The correct leader coaches and generates enthusiasm in the workplace and not by demanding that the followers go to yet another retreat or class on teambuilding.

In the canine world, the rules are simple: calm & assertive leaders create calm and engaged followers; the entire group (leaders/followers) follow the same rules and limitations on behavior, and the leaders coach the followers to be the leaders of tomorrow within the group and beyond. Successful human leadership requires these same operational elements.

If you are unsure of your leadership abilities, be around dogs, go to a shelter or even to a local dog park (without your own dog) and walk around the area. See which, if any, dogs begin to actually follow you; the dogs that read your energy or leadership as weak will not follow calmly. It is just that simple. Some of my clients are professional sports figures, millionaire owners of successful companies, Grammy award-winning artists and many more who are oviously good in their respective jobs yet don't understand leadership in their dogs' world. As soon as their leadership style changes at home with their dog, the humans become more productive and less stressed even in their work world, if they stay consistent. Consistency in leadership is strength and it is something the followers can always count on (which then becomes their comfort zone).

So take a hint from our dogs: stay calm and be a leader, not just a boss!

"Fred is the Dog Screamer."

Aggression and Calm/Assertive Correction

S arge is a 9-year-old Airedale from the Tampa area that was living with an elderly woman who passed away. His foster owners have been very good about wanting what is best for him even though they have been bitten by him on several occasions. This behavior and negative energy from him usually is centered around being wiped off with a towel. After taking him for a walk in the woods, we came across a dog he had always had problems with. I showed the owners how controlling their dog's state of mind and keeping them calm can actually control the other, more aggressive, dog. The other dog, even in his own yard, gave up barking and walked back into his porch.

Sarge did quite well on the walk, but his Kryptonite is the towel. His Pack Leaders usually try to do this inside the closed garage, which sometimes has its own negative energy that the dog will associate. My ultimate suggestion was to get him used to being calm around a towel by walking him while holding the towel on the same side as the leash, and perhaps even wiping him off in a different area (outside, for example). However, I wanted to have him work through his problems by being calm in the garage so I opted to work with him there.

He had a rather violent reaction to this, and tried to disagree with me by trying to bite me twice, which I recorded. However, dogs have to give respect and distance on their own, and while he tried to resist doing that, once I had his owner move away, he had to process that on his own. He also tried to bite me a third time (that did not get recorded, since I don't have a production staff!) and that required him to be placed on his side to calm down. He had so much negative energy that he stayed – on his own without any direction from me – for close to 20 minutes.

After that, we all went outside to throw the ball and have a different experience. I was able to stroke his head with the towel without his violent reaction, and the day ended on a positive note. The hardest thing for humans to do is to **NOT** hold a grudge against a dog for behaviors such as this, or to think that giving affection at the wrong time is going to "sooth the savage beast". In short, it will not. It WILL actually have the direct opposite response and can (and often does) result in a bite. Staying consistent with a more aggressive dog is a bit more challenging but we are working toward making the dog either adoptable or happier and calmer, which always gives us better behaviors.

Until the next time, stay calm and assertive even in the face of a violent outburst so that you can regain your leadership position with the dog.

UPDATE: Over the past month, Kamp K-9 Jax Bch and Koa have visited clients all over the state of Florida and the region, showing that balanced dogs are a possibility even in households where they never thought that to be possible with their dog. From March of 2015, Kamp K-9 Jax Bch has helped over 1000 Pack Leaders (this does not include students in my classes or attendees of the seminars) with dog psychology, aggression, too much energy, anti-social behavior and new pack member introductions (either dogs or new infants) all around the region. This is not to brag but it IS to show that there are a lot of misconceptions about how to treat dogs in the manner that shows them the MOST love and affection, after exercise and enforcing rules, boundaries, and limitations. Timing is everything, so make sure that you follow the formula and if you aren't getting the results you want, look to yourself first. Stay calm and assertive (firm). And, if you need help, ask for it to have a better, safer, and more comfortable life with your dog!

Consistent and Persistent

CONSISTENCY in leadership is just of the keys to success in the human world when it is imperative that the followers follow. And while Human Beings can be dangerous if unstable, dogs can also be dangerous when they are not given clear direction by a stable leader. Too often, when talking about dogs, we all are caught up with the concept of "alpha" leaders when in reality we're just talking about a balanced leader who is in charge. Would you ever dream of calling your supervisor an "alpha"? Probably not, and that's because it doesn't sound right; in fact, if your supervisor acted as an "alpha" in the sense that we usually use that term, chances are that you believe him or her to be unstable!

There are those born into a leadership role, and those who develop it over time – in humans and dogs. In addition, there are those who are NOT born to be anything BUT a follower… and then they get a dog, and sometimes a dog whose breed or demeanor dictates that they live with a strong and calm leader. That is where things go off the rails for everyone, because then the human is thrust into a position they are not comfortable with and they try their best but they have no real skills to deal with their new position in life. So it is with a dog who is thrust into that role by a human who was thrust into the role. And the cycle continues…

The dog can almost always change but can the human change? Absolutely! As a police and dog behavior trainer I have seen on countless occasions individuals who have been told that they can actually accomplish a difficult goal and then allowed to work in that direction to do some amazing things. However, **PERSISTENCE** is what is necessary and works hand in hand with **CONSISTENCY**. Is your dog having some setbacks in dog behavior? Awesome! That means you have the opportunity to work on your dog… and yourself! Investing in time with your dog means your dog sees that you are the kind-hearted leader who is going to take them places they can't (because they really can't!) imagine, and you get to see the possibilities really do exist.

However, trying to persist when you are not in the right frame of mind (calm/assertive – in charge and confident) just means that the consistency you are striving for is consistently doing it wrong! And your dog knows it long before you realize what is happening. Small steps for you and your dog are far better and more productive than one long session in the wrong state. When you and your dog came across each other, it was the start of a long relationship. So give it time.

Until the next time, stay consistent, persistent and focused to do it right!

How to Know When Your Dog is Having Fun!

S ome pack leaders are going to take offense with this chapter... simply because they misread their dog and I'm about to call them out on it. How would you respond if you were speaking with a stranger about playing a tennis match together and both of your respective dogs came up and said, "Hey, hey, hey! Knock that off. Don't do that! Come on, let's go!" and drug you off down the street! "But we were just getting ready to play!" you plead with your dog. "I want to go back," as you keep turning in the direction of your (now) lost playmate. How would YOU react to that?

How can you tell when your dog is having fun versus "being aggressive"? Many owners who have always owned dogs will still refer to the sounds and the behavior of their dogs as being aggressive. So what would you call football players? Aggressive or fun loving? In addition, why do we change the definition of the behavior based upon human or animal?

The answer lies in how we insert ourselves into the environment. If you like playing football, and you're good at it, you'll absolutely say you're having a great time. If you aren't good at it and everyone is running and hitting you, you will probably see it as a violent, aggressive game. Aggression is defined as a hostile action or behavior without provocation, which is not what spirited or excited behavior is. However, when that behavior stops being mutual and is more predatory then that is when it becomes aggression and requires correction.

The problem with most humans is that they are so afraid of their dog "embarrassing" them that they try to stop them from playing. That is what you do when you jump to conclusions without any basis other than your own potential embarrassment and fear.

When your dog chases a ball, are they having fun? Or is this simply a predatory behavior – hunting, chasing, catching, killing, and retrieving the prey for the pack leader? The answer is yes for both. You are feeding the instinct of the dog by that type of play and as long as this does not become obsessive, then the dog is being fulfilled.

The other point to make about whether your dog is having fun or being the bully is that you cannot correct behavior that has not happened; like in my example above. Alternatively, you get an opportunity to set and enforce rules when the unwanted behavior occurs so that you can correct and give boundaries for wanted behaviors, similar to raising a child. "Don't touch the stove; it's hot," you tell them. When do they learn? When they touch the stove, of course!

If you expect to have a misbehaving dog, the dog will fulfill your every wish and desire. The opposite is true, also. Treat your dog – and the people in your life – as though they have no limitations on what they do and how well they can perform, and I think you'll be amazed at the results. Until next time, go have fun!

Dog Aggression or Misdirected Energy?

A lfred is a 6-year-old miniature Poodle owned by a very nice lady. Alfred's story, however, is that he is dog aggressive and goes into a rage when other dogs are around. And, she was correct: I took Koa with me to work with Alfred and he definitely went after Koa and got corrected, once by me and once more a little later by Koa.

So Alfred got to come to Kamp K-9 Jax Bch for 12 days while his owner was out of town. I have a video that shows his actual entry into the area where the other dogs (Koa, Penny and Piper) were waiting patiently, and how – if the human pack leader is calm and assertive – the dogs will socialize better with no interpretation that they need to protect the pack leader or to BE the pack leader.

Alfred in his first 2 days was on pack walks, bike rides, treadmill walking, swimming in the pool and, most importantly, the dog park with a lot of other dogs. There was not one problem or disagreement out of him. Why? Rituals I have mentioned are important but he is not a dominant dog; he is nervous/anxious/tense which will result in aggression if not disagreed with by the Pack Leader. Or the other members of the pack. A dog like Alfred is happier when he is not in a role he is not designed for, as in leading the pack, or even being in the Happy-Go-Lucky middle of the pack. And when this happens, the pack is welcoming and nurturing to and for him. See his video here:

(https://www.youtube.com/watch?v=Xl8aAmgQDdw)

or click on the Kamp K-9 Jax Bch YouTube channel.

Since this is purely instinct and not training, you must first know about how dogs think and relate to others in a pack to determine what and how to change unwanted behavior. If you don't know, ask. If you do know, stay calm and assertive and help the pack!

?.!

ASK, TELL, COMMAND

One thing that some of my clients do not seem too clear on is how to tell their dog what they want them to do. Of course, I am not talking about the WORDS they use – your dog does not understand English, or Spanish, or Arabic, or any spoken language in the conventional human sense. They understand message intent and that is conveyed, just like in humans, by the two NON-VERBAL type of communication: body language and vocal inflection. The third component is actual words but in the human world, people only listen to 7% of what is said, 93% to the non-verbal communication. Your dog? Communication is 100% non-verbal. And it should be. No talking, control them by energy and body language.

I'm not saying that your dog doesn't understand what a repetitive sound means, I'm saying they did understand the sound until they connected it with a certain energy (body language) and message intent (vocal inflection). For example, the biggest mistake that all of us hear in the owners' message when their dog misbehaves is, "It's okay, don't be upset; there, there," etc., etc. The dog, however, hears no intensity of leadership behind that way of "direction" and therefore ignores the "commands". And the cycle continues and the behavior gets worse.

Even our well-behaved dogs need direction now and then, and sometimes they do not "listen" (by the way, they HEAR you; they just aren't impressed with your INTENT). There is a difference in how we say what we need to say and when, so let's take something from what I teach law enforcement officers about directing people in a way that they will understand what is meant, and how serious I am about it. It is three simple steps:

ASK, TELL, COMMAND. When you <u>ask</u>, when you <u>tell</u>, and when you <u>command</u> you use your voice in a distinctly different way. It's all about message intent. What happens when you only ASK for a behavior? Well, the answer might be, "No," and then what? The next step is TELL, as in, "I need you to do this." It's not a question but it's not a command. If the response to this is, "I'm not really interested in doing that," then the next escalated response by you is, "I need you to do this right now!" and your voice sounds different still. I am sure you are beginning to get the idea.

Can you start with a command? Sure, but the message and the response is immediately important. If your child was in the road with an approaching car, your message to get out of the road will need an immediate response because it is extremely important! It's also important to understand that not every direction is as important as the example I just gave. Like the cartoon at the beginning of this chapter, confusing and conflicting communication equals NO COMMUNICATION and means repeated unwanted behavior. Why? No clear direction by the Pack Leader. Remember that unclear direction to your dog is NOT leadership, and they will respond accordingly (weak energy by the human equals dominant behavior by the dog, which then becomes aggression). Dogs do not follow weak leaders.

Until next time, stay calm and communicate clearly!

Back to Basics: No Touch, No Talk, No Eye Contact?

I'd like you to meet Ebony, who acts like one of the Hounds of Hell. The depiction doesn't do her justice on the surface (although she IS a small black shepherd mix), but she DOES have three heads, just as in the drawing of the Hounds of Hell. Ebony was at the Humane Society as a hold, and now her owner could not be located. This might be just as well, because she is extremely unbalanced; she's fearful aggressive, generally didn't let anyone in or near her kennel, was housebroken but never got a chance to get out, and kept a steely gaze at your face while snarling, NOT at your feet or legs (which is not a normal behavior for any dog, let alone a shepherd mix).

So last week I saw her and thought it would be a nice challenge. Little did I know... It took 5 minutes to get her to calm down and somewhat go into avoidance, 5 more minutes to go into her kennel and get her to calm down, and then some more time to eventually have her calm enough when I presented the leash to be able to loop it over her head. All the while, being extremely upset over the process.

But staying calm with no talking is important when dealing with a dog with these issues. You won't be touching her anyway, and if you rush the process she will bite you and she <u>will</u> mean business. Eye contact, however, for this dog, is important because <u>she</u> has to break the gaze first, and every time. Why? Because she needs and wants a leader and she doesn't want to be in a leadership role, but she has to know that you respect her as a dog, and that you are willing to accept and safeguard her trust. Especially since she has gotten away with chasing humans off whom she does not trust or respect. Fearful aggression is vastly different from dominant aggression because being fearful indicates a lack of leadership in her world. Dominance means a challenge to leadership and almost always requires a different approach. But the respect and trust still must be a two-way street.

After getting the leash looped around her neck, I turned, opened our gate, and walked out. Ebony followed as if we had known each other all of her life without aggression or even a hint of what I had just experienced in very close quarters. She also pooped 4 times in the next hour and peed every chance she got. I worked with her for the next hour and she was just fine; in fact, sitting in the grass with her she would come up face to face with NO aggression whatsoever.

Until I put her back in the kennel. She did not want to stay and wanted to just walk out with me. I lead her back into her kennel a second time and readjusted the leash around her neck. MISTAKE! Ebony put her Hound of Hell mask back on, but this time she was within inches of me – I would have to neck bite her to get her to back up so I could leave. And I almost wasn't fast enough, but she did back away. I left and went around to the other side (where the public goes and the dogs can see better) and sat down on the floor facing sideways to her. She sidled up submissively as if to say, "Sorry, but I don't like it much in here," and then laid down on the other side of the gate but next to me.

A week later when I went back, the Behavior Manager asked if I could get her back out of her cage again because no one else could. I was surprised that she was still with us and of course said that I would. But here's where a global understanding of working with dogs through issues is vitally important. What I am doing with her is not new-fangled, or patently my technique, it is simply reading the dog and selecting the best course of action FOR HER.

While standing at her gate waiting for her to calm down, amidst the din of barking and uncontrolled walking of other dogs by staff handlers, I was looking at her with the calmest face I could muster no matter what she was throwing my way – because she clearly did not remember me. Another staff member came up behind me to tell me I shouldn't look at her in her eyes because that makes her worse. Remember, that when you are working a dog through dangerous issues, it's a good idea not to be distracted for obvious reasons. Another reason, however, is that if her aggression makes you back down then in her mind she got her way and it empowers her, thusly taking longer to start the process from the beginning.

After just responding with, "Yup," and not looking away, she interrupted me again. After advising her that I am the only one to have gotten her out of her cage in the past 2 weeks, and know what I am doing she suggested a treat reward instead, which also shows a grave misunderstanding of dogs in that state (which is why no one else has gotten her out). I dismissed that but telling her the nose does not engage during aggression and I appreciated her time but I had work to do. Ebony and I went through the same process as the last time (taking time, staying calm, no talking, lots of eye contact) until I could get close enough to loop the leash around her. This time I had a Chuck-it stick to extend my reach (my racket was at home) and it got stuck on the leash. Ebony wasn't happy with that at all and bit the crap out of that plastic stick – puncturing that hard plastic, as a matter of fact.

My second attempt was spot on and, just as the last time, as soon as the leash was on we walked out of the kennel with no problem – her behind me, no pulling, no barking, no biting. I spent more than 2 hours with her this time, walking all around, letting her poop 4-5 more times, getting her on the treadmill for a short period, walking around people, dogs, and things that I thought might spook her so we could work through them. The bottom line was that she was like a family pet (almost) and had no problem with any of it, including me bathing, drying, and brushing her. She even took a moment to give me lots of kisses.

Returning to the kennel was much better, but she still didn't want to stay (who can blame her?). After walking to the other side once again, she charged the fence like she always does but stopped much faster when she recognized my energy.

So, what do we take away from all of this? The No Touch, No Talk, No Eye Contact rules are not written in stone and are not for all occasions. It IS for meeting new dogs, even balanced ones, because it demonstrates where you are in the pack structure and where THEY are in the pack structure. But every dog is different, just as every human is different – not every fearful human is fearful for the same reason. Taking the time to observe, orient, decide, and act (known as the OODA Loop in the tactical world) helps us not only in dealing with humans, but also in dealing with the dogs we run across in our lives.

Lastly, what were the three heads of Ebony? One was Aggression, caused by the second head of Fear, and the third head eventually became Dog. But only through taking the time to work through issues, staying calm, and seeing all of her explosions of aggression as a call for help to humans willing to help in the best way FOR HER do we see Miss Dog come out and play.

Until the next time, stay focused on succeeding, and be persistent in your calm and assertive life even in the face of the Hounds of Hell!

UPDATE: After being out of her kennel and hanging around with staff in an office, Ebony tried to bite a volunteer as she walked away from Ebony to leave her in the office. She was euthanized the next day…

Back to Basics: Calm and Assertive

I n the previous chapter, you read about Ebony and how important it is to stay focused and persistent when you are working with an unbalanced dog. Like a paraphrased line from an obscure movie I saw recently, a dog is like a piano – if you keep banging on it and never give it the care required it gets out of tune. Then, someone has to come along and fine tune each string (230-250 of them!) one at a time before the entire instrument is whole again.

Dogs are like the piano in that sense. Keep banging away on an already out-of-tune dog and he will be badly out of tune. It also takes quite some time to get him back into tune and you must do it carefully and one "string" at a time. Yet, if it never gets entirely in tune and keeps being banged on, it will never be in tune until the entire system or environment changes. Thus, we have Ebony.

Now consider Ebony on steroids and you'll have Athena. Athena is another shelter dog, a large Great Dane mom, way too underweight and takes up the entire kennel (so no going in, really). And whose head was even with my waist. Athena was territorial and vocal when I passed by, so this is not Ebony – or any other dog. Every dog is different and each one will tell you what the problem is for him or her; you just have to listen with a canine ear, not a human one. In my past, I have owned Great Danes and other giant breeds and love working with them. However, although familiar I also respect the fact that they are dogs and, having been bitten badly by my own Great Dane in the past, these dogs are powerful.

I knew that the eye contact necessary with Ebony will never work for a territorial dog – you have to respect the fact that they are claiming their space and telling you about it. And warning you not to challenge them. Therefore, with Athena, I went to the open side and sat down right beside the fence facing 90 degrees away from her. Since she towered over even me when I was sitting down, she used that to her advantage and "whispered" in my ear at full volume that she was a force to be reckoned with and needed to be respected… and I did.

She very soon stopped barking and walked to the other side. I also walked around and opened the gate slowly but persistently to present myself and the leash but no talk and no eye contact. She came up to sniff the leash and I slowly looped it over her head, opened the gate fully and invited her out. Moreover, she and I became good buddies for the next hour. When I returned her back, she had no problem going in and she looked back as if to say, "Hey, thanks, bud."

The problem most of the time is that they are going back into an unstable environment, pianos constantly being banged on because of all of the barking and other instability. Thus, Ebony immediately reverted to Devil Dog behavior. Would Athena do the same thing when I saw her again?

The next day I had to be back there and decided, while I had a short period I could stay, to get Athena again. She was napping on the open side so I sat down quietly and let my scent and presence wake her gently. Which it did, but she was still a little startled to see someone there… and let me know it. But only once. Because this time I turned slowly and looked at her as if to say, "I'm your calm helper, returning to see you." Moreover, she walked to the other side and waited for me to get her!

How many different ways could that have gone? It should only go the most productive way for dogs and humans, and rushing isn't the answer at all. Thinking that because this dog is barking that she is like all dogs that bark is a recipe for failure and disaster. If you are a dog owner, a dog lover, or someone who just wants to know more about how to get along with dogs, keep reading this book and continue to interact – or watch interactions – with dogs. They teach us a lot; humans just don't pay attention most of the time.

Until next time, listen to your dog from a dog's point of view and you will understand their language even better than you do now!

Back to Basics:
Are You Social? Odds & Ends

J ust some odds and ends today, starting with **_Ebony_**. In a previous chapter I talked about Ebony and the behavioral problems she had. While she made very small improvements, Ebony was euthanized after several outbursts she had while being cared for in a calm state with other members of the Humane Society staff. The reason I am sharing this with everyone is to remind people of a couple of really important points. One, the Humane Society is NOT set up to be a dog psychology center where dogs get "fixed" with behavior problems. There are many dogs there that need good homes that are not problems and are awaiting their forever pack leader to find them. Second, people (as in Ebony's owner) made her what she was because I am sure she was not born like that. But she became that with a lot of work/neglect/affection at the wrong time/no affection – whatever the combination was, it was wrong because she became fearful and aggressive. Giving affection at the wrong time nurtures a poor state of mind for the dog and is not good for them in the long run, either. If you know of someone whose dogs are exhibiting problems with their behavior, seek professional help – if it's not me, please select someone who knows dogs and how THEY think and doesn't just teach "tricks". *Trainers* generally do not do behavior rehabilitation and also usually do not change the human component, which is where the poor behavior originates.

Social Dogs: I recently worked with a Rhodesian Ridgeback/Weimaraner mix who was extremely aggressive and attacked several dogs and almost their owners. This poor guy was always being avoided by the neighborhood (understandably so!) and his owners also avoided all contact with other dogs while on the walk. After showing them how to have their dog respectfully meet another dog (namely, his nemesis – another Weimaraner) we all walked the neighborhood with both dogs walking side by side with their owners, dealt with another dominant small dog with no outbursts, and left on a positive note. The lesson? Don't give your dog limitations that he or she doesn't have, stay calm when they get upset, choose to see a particular POSITIVE outcome, don't live in the past and always end on the positive behavior you want to have repeated the next time. As always, however, after I show the owners that their dog can do it, it is up to them to continue the work. If you always avoid having your dog meet another dog, what message are you sending? If you always require that your dog meet all dogs respectfully, what message are you sending? It is that simple.

Behavior Mirroring: A little self-analysis test for you! What is it that you see in your dog's behavior that you don't like? Once that question is answered ask yourself, "What am I doing to cause this?" Because 9 times out of 10, well-intentioned and loving dog owners ARE the problem; something is off about what they are doing and it's a relatively easy fix when someone can point it out to them. But you have to think like the dog or at least respect the mind of the dog! Don't be afraid to ask for help or advice – this is affection for your dog, also!

Obsessive Behavior: There's probably nothing worse than going with your favorite pooch to the dog park to throw the ball and have some big, huge dog jumping at the ball in your hand. Often we create more bad behavior by trying to play "keep away" by turning away or jerking the ball away or both. Both of which can get you hurt – perhaps not intentionally but you are creating a prey drive in that dog and he or she is not being given rules/boundaries/limitations with play time. The reward for CALM behavior WITH RESPECTFUL SPACE is to throw the ball so that the relationship is calm behavior means reward rather than throwing it just to get them away from you... you know they're coming back, right?! Expect to see and work towards the correct behavior and don't reward bad behavior.

Owning a Dog: Owning a dog is a multi-year commitment to walking, training, directing, and loving your dog who is going to be your shadow for many years to come. And many of us wouldn't have it any other way. The years of my life where I didn't have a dog were times where something was missing. Now, I can't think of not having Koa to have as my companion during the day and when we travel, as well as helping me with the dogs I work with. What I'm saying here is owning a dog can be a lot of work but do it right or don't bother to get a dog. Also, many dogs in the shelter didn't necessarily have a bad life or get abused – their owners just couldn't care for them the way they should be cared for, or their situation changed drastically which precluded them from owning their dog. I would rather have someone make the decision to give up their dog than to have the dog neglected, abused, and eventually die because the human was too prideful to do what is right for the animal. And, there are plenty of good dogs at the shelter for anyone who's looking (I'm just saying).

Until next time, remember that **affection** also means making sure that your dog is social, behaves appropriately, and is calm. That can only happen if YOU are social, behave appropriately, and are calm. Then, give your dog as much affection as they, and you, can stand!

Back to Basics: Let Go!

S ince we're out of town in a dog (mostly) unfriendly area of Florida and Koa had to stick around back home, I found a flock of pelicans early one morning who were fishing and hanging out, and it reminded me of something important to discuss. Why can't animals emotionally live in the past? Because every single day they have to work towards life and living, eating, playing, socializing – all of the things that prolong life, not shorten it. It's in their DNA, a requirement in their lives to move forward, not backward. Letting go is something that many humans (me, included) find difficult to do. Letting go of the bad, scary, and horrible experiences that we have gone through. Sometimes humans even do this with their dogs' lives – emotionally remember and relive the bad, horrible things they may have gone through. What humans forget is that it's not healthy for us to hang on to our own past, and it is really unhealthy to hang on to what we think is our dogs' past. Why? Because it makes us weak, in our dogs' eyes, and that creates behavior problems because now the dog believes that it needs to protect the human. Not some of the time. <u>All</u> of the time.

Without exception, every dog I've worked with has an owner that will tell his or her back story as a reason for whatever the unwanted behavior might be. These very loving dog owners are inadvertently creating the behavior they don't want by their energy they possess based on the story. While I am honored to work alongside these incredible dog lovers, I also know that listening to the story for the dog's sake is exactly the wrong thing for me to do when I get to meet the dog. I listen to help the <u>human</u> get past the past. Most dogs will tell a different story from a different perspective than their owners, and have a different set of goals than the human might want or believe.

So why does it look like "magic" when I correct unwanted behavior and get the desired response, or when I don't get a chance to even see the unwanted behavior without the owner present? Because I don't share that past with the dog, I'm sharing what we are doing right then – playing, walking, hanging out. Then we get back with the owners so that I can see the behavior change; and then the dog tells me what the problem is. The humans have forgotten to "let go" of what keeps them, and their dogs, from excelling.

Coaching people is what I have done for a long career – not sports, exactly, but behavior coaching which has a direct correlation to outstanding performance. It's just that dogs will show your progress with them light years faster than a human experience ever will.

Until next time, stay calm and let go!

Back to Basics: Leadership (and Consequences) Within the Pack

In one of my earliest posts, I talked about the pack within the pack, discussing studies done in Hungary with a pack of off leash Vizslas and how the dog pack leader changes during playtime determining the direction the rest of the pack. I have also written about how, within the pack, there are leaders, followers, and the intermediaries and each has a specific job (followers are rear security, leaders choose the direction, intermediaries keep the pack together, happy and moving in the right direction).

Beyond that discussion, let's talk about human pack structure within a dog pack. The human is the pack leader, but within a structure which is limited in its scope. For example, where there are a pack of dogs and humans walking there are sub-packs within the pack. Koa and I are a pack; Dan and MC are a pack; Margo and Elvis are a pack; Mike and Atticus are a pack; and so on. We are primarily responsible for our sub-pack but have a responsibility to assist another pack leader only when it's warranted. If the play with all of the dogs becomes too rough, all pack leaders who are closest are empowered to make the corrections to whomever they choose to reclaim a balanced environment and to separate the parties while the other pack leaders are making their way in that direction to reclaim their pack. This has happened where because of distance one of us in the pack is the closest and best choice for correction without favoritism – even if it is our dog, we make the correction for pack balance and leadership cohesion. It is a simple chain of command.

However, if Koa has decided to stray for a moment it is my responsibility to make the correction verbally or otherwise without participation by the other pack leaders. Should Mike try to correct Koa in this instance it is viewed in the dog world as a direct challenge, or an attempt to launch a coup, to the leadership position of that pack leader. And it would force me to repel this challenge in the harshest manner possible. In the animal world this attempt to challenge throws potential confusion into the dog's mind (especially if they are not balanced) and causes the dog to wonder, "Who's in charge here?" The answer comes in the response of the pack leader.

In the dog world, a direct challenge, or an attempt to overthrow the leader by "bossing" THEIR subordinates around is a very big deal and results in only a few, but very harsh and often not survivable, conclusions. The first outcome is that the original leader either gives in to the challenge or is defeated because they are too tired or too old to fight, which always results in the death of that ostracized leader because they are removed from the pack and are no longer a part. The second outcome is that the challenger is defeated and this may result in the same outcome – IF the challenger can run fast enough. If not, they are killed for the sake of the pack's survival and unit cohesion; there is no recidivism. Simple as that.

Therefore, it is not the action but the consequences of that action that determine the strength of the leadership position. If you think about it, it is really no different in your own employment world. Dissenters and challengers either defeat their opponents or are sent to Siberia (figuratively, unless you're in Russia, in which case it is literally!). Furthermore, the defeat of the challenger serves as a message to the dog that 1) the pack leader is truly in charge, 2) it's not a good idea to challenge the pack leader unless you KNOW you're going to win, and 3) the "street credibility" of the pack leader has just increased exponentially because the pack is assured that they are safe and have the right pack leader for them.

Until next time, study your own pack and be the best pack leader for your sub-pack member!

Back to Basics: Socialization

Socialization is the process by which an individual learns the values, behaviors, and social skills, appropriate to their environment and society. If you have been reading this book, you will already know that the earliest you can have your dog experience the outside world, with your calm demeanor showing them that they have nothing to fear, the better your dog will be when interacting with the outside world.

This includes other dogs. The earlier you can let them be around other dogs, especially balanced ones, the better. But what if that's not what happened with the dog you have now? There are a variety of reasons why this happened and that part is not important. What IS important is that you remain calm and consistent in your work with your dog and know that sometimes it might just take longer. Ultimately, it is YOU that will take your dog to the highest point you can; not trainers, not tons of money, only you, their owner and pack leader.

We would all LOVE to have our dogs be social but ask yourself this question: Are you social, display appropriate behaviors, and do you stay calm? If not, then you cannot expect your dog to be social, display appropriate behaviors, or stay calm in a social setting. The dog is a little furry behavioral mirror of ourselves. It always amazes me when I see an anti-social person with a dog that is social. That makes for an awesome dog! But it's also a little troubling because the fact is if they live with instability they themselves will become unstable, eventually.

It also amazes me that these same people with that kind of demeanor are confused about why their dog might misbehave in a social setting, as if it's only the dog. Or the dog's back story. Or someone else's fault.

I am working with a family that has a situation totally different. I was contacted after their newly acquired large breed dog, a 9-year old Airedale who is a rescue, had a major altercation with the neighbor's dog. She apparently had not been socialized, had not had a social life, and the owners weren't sure if it was a great idea to keep her. After helping them originally on learning how to walk a large breed, I also enlisted the help of my best helper, Koa. After a short little explosion in his direction, she got over it and eventually walked beside and roamed around in her yard unleashed without an issue.

However, once she met all of us on our morning walk, she went after not one, not two, but four different dogs including Koa. Although she will be the subject of the work I'll be doing with her while she stays at Kamp K-9 Jax Bch for 10 days, the short answer for her behavior, I believe, is that she has never gotten the chance to be a dog and have fun. She is constantly on the lookout for a chance to bite another dog and perhaps smaller beings (which is a concern for the owners' great-grandchildren's' safety) in a calculated "sneak attack" mode. Otherwise a sweet dog, her owners now are of a mind that they will do whatever it takes to rehabilitate her. And you can see it in their demeanor – much more in charge than before and taking a true leadership role, which you can see in the dog's slight change in behavior. But after 9 years of being a certain way, it will take a bit more intense work to get her happy with life, instead of constantly looking for the fight.

Remember, the most love you can show to your dog is that you will invest however much time it takes to make them happy and social. Stay tuned for her progress, which I will share with you, as well as hers (and my) successes and failures, and until the next time stay calm and social!

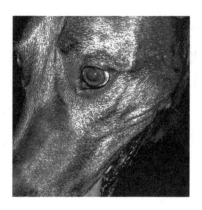

Pent-up Energy and Your Inner Pack Leader

As you are probably aware, Hurricane Matthew scraped the Florida east coast last week. For those who stayed, many people spent all of Friday secured in their homes. After the storm passed on Friday evening, Saturday dawned bright and sunny and besides the cleanup time, many also ventured out to area restaurants. The interesting thing was that the news outlets labeled that as "cabin fever" where people had to get out of the house because they were "cooped up". But that was only for one day! As this is a common problem with dog owners, let's explore "being cooped up". Especially when, for a dog, this means they'll be getting into trouble by doing destructive things.

When your dog is home all day long and is let out into a yard we view that as giving them exercise so they can run off their pent-up energy and clear their mind. The question is, don't people have yards to go out into and clear their minds and bodies of the excess energy? The answer, of course, is yes but – you might say – it's different for my dog than for me. And you are exactly correct! Your dog actually needs MORE time than we need to feel less stressed and clear minded. In fact, those of us who live in apartments or condos have dogs that get far more exercise than those with yards because they HAVE to get their dogs outside and walking.

We have activities that we can do in the house if we are stuck inside for an extended period of time: television, radio, video games, books, activities such as cleaning the house and rearranging things, etc. What does your dog have? IF you throw the ball for him or her in the house, that's only one activity; chewing a toy also only lasts so long. All of the things we usually equate with helping the dog with their energy are usually one-dimensional. But real pack leaders take care of their pack; they know what they truly need and when they might need it.

The Walk is foundational for leadership but it also acts as a mental and physical challenge to our dogs. Simply walking down the street is not necessarily a challenge (sometimes it's more of a challenge to the humans!) without rules/boundaries/limitations and being imaginative on your walk. Don't always go the same direction or path, mix it up a bit. If you can, do your walking on a nearby trail or park. If you also have to get out of the house for a break, take your pack member with you and find a dog friendly location to shop or eat (or walk). Challenge yourself, and your dog will tell you whether or not it's a challenge to them.

Remember that our dogs want to follow a calm and confident leader. If you are that leader your dog will let you know; if you're not, your dog will also let you know that! When owners tell me that they have a very intelligent dog, "BUT," then I know that the "intelligence" of the dog came out when the human connected on a canine level or when they didn't. Now the trick is to stay connected and it starts by staying connected with your pack leader self.

Until the next time, stay calm and connected to your inner pack leader!

The Most Basic Misunderstanding

While I have been preparing for the "How to be an Even Better Pack Leader" class event coming up in a couple of weeks, I have had the opportunity to speak with more owners than usual about their dogs and the specific problems they may have. We have over 100 people signed up for this event, which means there is a lot of interest in the material but – more importantly – a lot of caring for their dogs. The vast majority of conversations have a component of, "I know it's me and not the dog," which is an incredibly wonderful proclamation because it means these pack leaders' minds are open to learning more about what they might not realize they know.

Many of the folks I work with can do the same things I show them that their dog can do, they just didn't realize that was the language they needed to "speak" to their dog. In other words, the language we need to use with our dogs doesn't involve a lot of sound, and it absolutely doesn't require talking in the conventional sense.

Animals speak to each other through their energy. Our cat, Shaka, is a pack member in our house and he is as off limits to aggression as any other member of the pack. He will "tell" a boarder at the house when they are too close, wrong energy, correct energy, and has no problem walking among the pack. Which at any given time has been as many as five different dogs. He also knows that while I'll let him speak to the energy, just as I'll let the dogs speak to it, I am the one still in charge so that if any of the pack members are out of line, I'll be disagreeing with it. If not, THEY become the pack leader.

What is the basic misunderstanding that humans have? The role of a pack leader. Pack leaders serve two main functions: Protection & Direction. I provide protection from the wrong energy or incorrect disagreements within the pack. Because of this, I gain more trust, respect, and loyalty from the other members. I also provide direction, the "what are we doing next?" component. Again, more trust, respect, and loyalty. When your dog gets so excited to go on a walk that they pull you out the door, you shouldn't be surprised that they will get more aggressive towards people or dogs on the walk because who is providing direction? They are. They are now also providing protection because you did not assume the role of the leader – you allowed them to take over. When you try to regain control, it becomes harder because you are now CHALLENGING the pack leader's authority and it now probably involves frustration, stress, anger, embarrassment on your part. Here's a hint: preventing this behavior from the beginning by calmly asserting yourself as the leader before you even pick up the leash in the house is the key.

By the way, the caption for the accompanying photo found on the internet says, "Walking a dog is an easy thing to do. Just follow his lead." And they were serious!

Until the next time, stay calm and keep learning!

Meet Anxious Mason

Mason is a shelter dog at the Jacksonville Humane Society and was labeled as "extremely timid". You would be, too, if you had to listen to all that barking every day. I noticed one of the high school community service walkers CARRYING this guy from one of the yards earlier in the day (he's not small).

His card says that he has to be carried into and out of his kennel and carried out of the yard, just like I saw. Of course, I like a challenge so the afternoon walk was the chance to meet him and work with him. And I wasn't going to lose.

One of the absolute best things about volunteering there is that I get to see firsthand what techniques work and which ones don't. Here's the biggest tip: respect animal/dog first, and then take your time and be patient. And yes, Mason was bad – on a 1-10 scale of anxiety he was an 8 or 9. He would shut down when the gate was opened. So I spent about 10 minutes earning his trust and his respect by showing the same to him.

When it came time to take him out, he positively shut down at the opening, laying all of the way down and not budging. I sat on the floor of the hallway and kept constant pressure on the leash to get him to snap out and after about 15 seconds he got up and walked to my side. We had several other chances to correct that state of mind and each time it took less and less time until we walked all over the compound. He would stop every so often and lay in the grass (awesome!) and I eventually got him to jump up on the deck, which he absolutely wouldn't do at first. That took about 15 seconds...

Much happier afterwards, he walked proudly into his kennel and got treats and lots of affection. I did leave a note to be patient and STOP PICKING HIM UP! Calm, assertive RESPECT is the key.

What does "Assertive" mean?

I n another chapter, I talked about being the leader you need to be for your group or pack. The problem is that many humans make that whole concept hard to apply because they think they have to be something they're not. Often, when my clients try to do this, the dog knows better than to follow a poser and they rebel. Being assertive is nothing more than being "in charge". Simply put, if you are not in charge someone will be and if you are thinking in terms of relating to a dog, if it's not you, it's the dog.

So let's see some examples of being assertive and how easy it is to have the dog change when the authority figure is both calm and assertive:

How do you walk with a dog off leash? Leadership, and calm & assertive discipline when necessary. And practice

trusting that your dog will follow the leader. Koa always gets reinforcement in this. When he was younger, he was about 70% good about this; then he would go off on a tangent (we used to joke that he was a truancy dog because he would always gravitate toward the kids that skip school

in the morning and go to the beach). Now, he is very good at following in a less independent way. Practice takes place when you walk with your dog with a loose leash or even a long leash but you are not having to leash correct your dog. Loose leash is the next best thing to off leash.

This little pack leader was the almost 2-year-old next door neighbor to a client I was working with, along with her energetic 9-month old pup, Sydney. The little girl was so enamored with the dog as they were passing by that she wanted to pet Sydney and then wanted to hold the leash. Usually, that would be a cause for attention and caution, but as Sydney got closer she started licking the little one. When she did the typical human thing (try to shy away from that energy), I told her to just tell Sydney, "No!" in a quiet way. She immediately did it like a true pack leader (pointing at her and Sydney instantly got the message). From there, it was obviously natural for her to

walk around the driveway and hold the leash but it clearly wasn't required. I have 10 more photos or her being followed by Sydney with no further correction. By the way, that's a 15-foot leash you see in the photo and it wasn't needed at all. Way to go, little Pack Leader!

One of these dogs I think you know. The one on the outside is Maya, who supposedly had trouble walking without pulling. It never recurred after the first, very light, leash correction. The one in the middle is a Spaniel named Marley. Marley's long time housemate had died 2 weeks before and it was traumatic for the humans. They began seeing that Marley was withdrawn where he used to be bubbly and energetic but since I was not working with the family and only keeping Marley for daycare, they didn't get the benefit of having the education about dog psychology. Marley was also supposedly skittish around other dogs and people. As you can see, aside from the fact that Marley was fine around everyone else, the pack – and the power of the pack – helped Marley be just fine, which is why I put him in the middle of 2 very balanced dogs. In fact, the grief and sadness in the human house was affecting Marley and his humans continued to make their reality HIS reality. The very second he was removed from that environment with calm, assertive and balanced interaction he changed. That's the beauty of working with dogs.

Until the next time, be the calm authority figure your dog is looking – and hoping – for!

Is This Okay?

A short chapter today to help some dog owners experience rough play vs. aggression. There is a video on my YouTube channel that acts as a short tutorial just to get the ball rolling about dogs biting each other during play.

Okay, so since you know that dogs don't have hands, they have to manipulate their world somehow, right? Imagine yourself without arms trying to wrestle with someone else without arms. How easy would that be? And how soon would it be before YOU started using your mouth?

This is certainly not to say that pack leaders shouldn't monitor the play. It IS your job to supervise the level of the intensity that goes along with play. It is no different than when a child is getting too active when they're playing and it looks like they're beginning to lose control. Pack leaders should understand this principal and also the fact that all pack leaders can and should control the intensity of group dog play.

If you are truly unsure, especially with your dog, here are a few tips that can help:

1. If your dog has had an "incident" in the past, leave the past behind. Your dog probably did (they usually do!).
2. Ask a professional WITH EXPERIENCE to accompany you to the dog park to help explain what you are seeing.
3. Go to the dog park without your dog and just watch how the dogs – and humans – interact. Did a dog come into the park in an excited state or did the pack leader wait for a calmer state of mind before entering ahead of the dog? Is there a lot of tension/frustration/anxiety on the part of the human? All of these can signal a potential outburst.
4. If a fight does break out, listen to the humans, not the dogs. This is where many humans cannot control their emotions. Watch what the response is to the "fight"; did they simply leash up their dog and remove them from the park? This is not always the best response and does show a lack of leadership on the part of the human.

Until the next time, stay calm, assertive, and be the Pack Leader your dog needs!

How BIG Does a Pack Leader Need to Be?

Pack Leaders come in all shapes and sizes. Occasionally I work with families where the little ones are around. I don't mind having them participate for a number of reasons, and here are two big ones.

First, they don't live the same back-story their parents sometimes do about the dog and what they've gone through in life. Children really do "live in the moment" and so their energy tends to be a little more real and much less stressed.

Second, and probably most importantly, they will become tomorrow's balanced pack leaders if they are allowed to exercise their abilities with dogs. For example, my niece is a pack leader in how she directs and controls her dog. Granted, Nathan is small but how many adults do you see pulled around by their small dogs that are out of control?

Another example is friends of ours who have three

daughters, who Koa probably outweighs with their weights combined! However, even in a very public place with many distractions, Leah is handling herself – and Koa – quite well!

When you look at all of the pictures, you will see what I try to teach adults who might be having problems with their

walks: loose leash, comfortable body language, calm/assertive demeanor, and enjoy the walk! Remember that YOU are walking and the dog is accompanying you; you are not "walking the dog". It's a matter of perception, but a powerful conversation you should be having with yourself. If you are walking the dog, then it is no wonder the dog wants to do what it wants to do and you are just along for the ride… or the pull!

On the other hand, these photos should indicate that the girls are all taking a walk with a companion but there is no dispute who is in charge and control.

Until next time, stay calm and enjoy your walk!

Dog Park Energy

As Pack Leaders, our responsibility is to our pack, to house and feed them, love them, and to keep them safe in a smart, Pack Leader way. This includes taking them out of the home, into crowds, the beach, and dog parks. Keeping them safe doesn't mean picking them up when YOU are afraid (that's a GREAT way to get bitten, even by your own dog). It means not placing them in a situation that could be a danger to them, and this has to do with reading Dog Behavior/Body Language.

While that will be the subject of a chapter, reading dog behavior will go a long way towards keeping everyone safe. Rough play is essential in the dog world and if you're unsure about which is aggression and which is rough play then study other dogs, too. It's always a question of what is the right thing to do when you arrive at the dog park and start reading the energy inside. And the short answer to this is simply don't go into the dog park if you don't think it's a good idea. Once inside, it becomes not the other dog owner's responsibility but ALL OF THE PACK LEADERS' responsibility to control behavior. An owner who doesn't understand this probably already has a dog that is a problem so it should be easy to spot. And if you are unable or unwilling to do this, don't go in.

Another option besides not going in is to go to another portion of the park and look for the dogs/owners who are calm and balanced. Projecting calm, in-control energy on your part also sends a message to the other dogs that you are an authority figure. If you cannot do this, please do your dog a favor and find another outlet for their energy. Most dogs can get along just fine when we leave them to their own devices and control the boundaries of good behavior (we do it with our children; our dogs are no different). If things are getting out of hand and no one is controlling it, do what ALL dogs do – if there is a hole in the leadership hierarchy, FILL IT YOURSELF!

Good dog owners know this and don't take things personal when a leader steps in and makes sure things don't get out of hand. And, timed well, this leadership behavior is powerful in the human as well as dog world.

Until next time, protect your canine but let them be dogs, too!

Fulfilling Your Pack Member

M any behavioral issues that I see and that I read about come from anxiety and pent-up energy that is not drained. It's not that the owner doesn't love their dog; it's just that they aren't sure how to love them the right way FOR THE DOG'S SAKE.

When the formula of Exercise, Discipline, and then Affection is used, your dog is fulfilled... yes, it IS that simple! But "The Walk" is a mental exercise for most breeds. Small dogs, those with shorter legs, and those that are low energy do not need strenuous exercise every day and The Walk can provide the draining of energy that the dogs and owners need. Other breeds, and certain aged dogs, need to have their energy drained differently – if you think you can keep up with most any high-energy dog on a run, then you are delusional! Even the fastest man alive has trouble breathing the dust of a greyhound! A bike, roller blades, skateboards, or learning the correct way to put your dog on a treadmill are excellent ways for everyone to get their daily exercise.

Another way for them to truly be fulfilled is allowing them to social with other members of their species. Dog parks, beaches, simple walks, can all contribute to their socialization and makes you a stronger pack leader. Remember that your energy – negative or positive – will dictate the outcome to any meeting. If you are nervous, anxious, fearful, frustrated then guess what your dog will be feeling? Being confident, self-assured, calm, assertive, in control of yourself and your emotions – in other words, characteristics of a leader even under fire – will assure that your dog will respect and follow that energy to the ends of the earth.

Most people in leadership positions in the human world are unhealthy and unhappy when they micromanage everything an employee or a subordinate does. They don't enjoy the ride, so to speak. I've worked for people like that and I'm sure you have, too. Well, the same goes for Pack Leader behavior – are you enjoying the ride/the walk/ the exercise/being with your furry companion? If you aren't, I guarantee the dog knows... the dog always knows because he or she is more attuned to us than we are to them. They watch, they study, they just KNOW through instinct. Ever been really upset and have your pack member try to comfort you without being asked? They know...

Lastly, make sure that your dog gets to do something you know they enjoy, just for them. A favorite chew, an interaction with a particular dog or dogs, etc. For Koa, it

is holes at the beach and it doesn't matter what size. We may be on a pack walk, but for his sake, and sometimes for mine, we'll seek out holes for him to lay in and enjoy life and the creations around us. This is one that we found and it gives you an idea of how deep it was… he completely disappears from view!

This week our family is going to Sarasota to visit family but also to where Venice Beach has an off-leash dog park, also known as "The Happiest Place on Earth (for dogs!)" (Sorry, Walt Disney). Therefore, that is where Koa will spend part of his (and my) time. Until the next time, enjoy the ride and fulfill your pack members – all of them!

The Power of the Pack

Cesar Millan talks extensively about the power of the pack; the ability for the pack to do what humans cannot, no matter how smart or loving we are. Sometimes we have to let the pack do the work they are intended to do...

A balanced pack can bring an unbalanced dog into their folds very quickly, with a few exceptions. One is where the pack recognizes a truly bad energy from the new member and decides that is not for them. They will usually walk away from the unbalanced energy and extend no invitations to play or to roam with the pack. This means there is some work to do from the pack leader with balancing whatever the issue is with the individual dog.

A second exception is where the new dog is not aggressive, but fearful/dominant and that affects their ability to walk with the pack. Kobe was one such dog. A Havanese, he would act dominant until he got around the rest of the pack then he would distance himself while acting as though he was the leader. The pack would walk away from him which he was constantly confused about.

Eventually, both Koa and MC would "bat" at his butt, something I had not seen either dog do to any other dog... and while Remy (calm/submissive) was right next to him on the walk, they would only do that to Kobe. In fact, whenever he would fall behind, they would go back to him and start prodding him along physically.

I eventually realized that this was something humans do in a different way when we want someone to either play or "get in the game". When I came to this realization I stopped controlling the intensity of the prodding and Kobe started not only playing but inviting others to play. Granted it took 2 weeks, but the pack accomplished what humans cannot because we read things differently and handle things in a less primal way.

The Dog You Need

Although I have written about this before on another level, a recent recurring theme in my training from clients is, "Our other dog was NEVER like this one." As the saying goes, "You get the dog you need, not the dog you want." Many times, we have forgotten that no dog is exactly what you want behaviorally all of the time.

First of all, they are different animals just as humans are different from one to another. Second, we have often forgotten what it took to get the previous dogs' behavior in line and the fact that they may be aged, or have already passed over the Rainbow Bridge, by the time we get our next dog. Older dogs are usually more balanced because they are used to being calmer.

And then we get a puppy! With LOTS of energy! Which puppies naturally have, and sometimes we don't do our homework to select a breed and an energy that will fit our lifestyle. We see the cute puppy (they are ALL cute, by the way; so NO, you can't take them *all* home) and we start the humanization process which leads us to bring the dog home and give them LOTS of love with no rules.

The rules start the second you and your dog meet. And when you have selected the one you WANT (note that emphasis?) you begin by introducing leashes and introductions to your house and the rest of your pack. Things can go very badly when your pack, humans included, don't have rules/boundaries/limitations to live by.

I often hear from humans that are starting to see aggression either in the house or on walks, that their dogs were fine for a time, "And then, all of a sudden, they changed." Almost always this can be traced back to a change in the humans or in the human environment. When I ask how they are on the walk I also hear, "We don't walk anymore because they pull too much or they're too reactive to other things." And so the spiral continues until it gets out of hand.

In the previous chapters, you've seen that The Walk is about leadership and not necessarily exercise. No leadership from the pack leader? The dog will fill the void you created and it usually won't end well. Our happy followers are, in essence, being abused by our lack of commitment to walk them and be a leader. Every walk is your chance to reinforce to your dog(s), and to you, that you are the leader and that you are a GOOD and calm leader.

There is no Easy Button in this life, and that extends to your dogs. You have to put in the work to get results. We had a huge pack walk at last night's Canine Leadership Course graduation that included 17 people and 11 dogs, all without the first problem. One of my new pack leaders remarked, "This stuff really works! It really does!" But that is ONLY accomplished through the work and dedication to our dogs, and that is how we grow as a pack leader and as a person. The dog is there to also improve YOU, and sometimes we need more improvement than other times. This may be one of those times.

Lisa likes to equate how different we are from being young to when we are older as, "God is pruning us just like we do a tree to make it a better and more productive tree." Could it be that this wonderful animal that can cause us so much frustration is a pruning shear put here for you? I like to think so…

Until next time, stay calm and keep pruning!

Introducing Your Human Self to a Dog like a real Pack Leader

Here are three things everyone NEEDS to know about introducing yourself to a dog.

The other day, Parker, a Great Pyrenees, came to Kamp K-9 Jax Bch while his owners were out of town. Parker is a little more nervous and skittish around new things, sounds, people, etc. Dogs like Parker need to have their self-esteem as a dog empowered and it usually takes a little longer with them than even an aggressive dog. While Parker and I were walking down the street, we came across some high school girls walking in the neighborhood, and all of them wanted to see and pet him. While he is a beautiful dog, a respectful introduction from humans is always necessary, no matter the dog/breed/temperament.

One girl asked if it was okay to pet him. I told her it was, but to simply stand straight with her arms by her side and let him sniff her first. Instead, she did the same thing that all uneducated dog lovers do: she bent way over and stuck her hand in his face. I told her 2 more times to stop before her friends finally told her, "He said just stand there and let the dog sniff you!" She finally straightened up, Parker sniffed her, and after a few seconds he ignored the rest of the contact, a clear signal that this was okay.

This girl – and many well-intentioned humans – was under the misconception that if you want to meet a dog, you have to present your hand for them to smell. Because of a dogs' olfactory capabilities, they can smell you from quite a distance, so the close sniffing becomes an effort to identify scent with energy. They then decide whether you are a threat to them, or whether or not they like your energy, and then they walk away. A dog that walks away and turns their back on you has given you the message, "I don't feel threatened by you."

Another misconception is that we go TO the dog, whereas in the pack world dogs come to us to sniff because that is what a respectful follower does. Pack leaders do not go to followers and say, "Let me give you affection and excitement, you wonderful subordinate." That behavior, in fact, shows the dog how little you understand their interaction with leaders and just what your status is as a leader (um, you're NOT!)

Lastly, think of what the dog sees from their perspective. Look at the accompanying photo. Here is Parker having a hand stuck in his face and he looks neither happy nor comfortable. Then look at Lisa. SHE'S happy to see the dog but what does the dog see? Fingers (also known as "something to bite") and excitement, which some dogs will see as too much too soon and will disagree with that energy usually with a growl or a snap. If Parker were a different or more aggressive dog, this look will be a prelude to a bite and is a warning to the offender (which most dog lovers miss). Petting the dog under the chin after he/she has made their decision about you is truly more respectful in their eyes, and can mitigate the damage of a bite should you misread the dog.

Most dogs are happy-go-lucky and therefore this may not necessarily be an issue. Nevertheless, you can establish yourself as a pack leader by showing respect in the eyes of even the more distrustful dog by understanding and learning how to introduce yourself, and you can be around many types of personalities of dogs and stay safer and in control. Regardless, if you want to establish yourself as a pack leader, it starts from the first contact.

Until the next time, stay Calm, Assertive, and Respectful! And by all means, teach others how to respectfully meet dogs!

Is It Possible?

This Thanksgiving I was reminded of how thankful I am to have dogs in my life, and how thankful I am to have A LOT of dogs in my life. Thanksgiving weekend brought 4 additional dogs – bringing the total in the house to 5 – all from different walks of life, different breeds, different sizes, different ages (the oldest is 15!) and different energy levels (and no rehab: this was Thanksgiving, after all). Moreover, all of the dogs got along as if they've always lived with each other. How? By the Pack Leaders bringing BALANCE and calm, assertive energy into the equation from the dog point of view. Was it balanced from the very beginning of their stay? No, but each brought a balance of sorts when they came by. It doesn't mean they don't have a personality of their own. What's the goal? We want the personalities to stay the same, but everyone is balanced about it.

A couple of them had to be corrected at first, not because of bad behavior but behavior that didn't conform to the rules/boundaries/limitations in this house, and those are rules that HAVE to be there with 5 dogs and a lot of cooking going on before visitors come calling. Visitors in the form of my son and their year old "I don't have to do what you tell me to do" puppy. As usual, the balanced dogs took the reins to correct behavior instead of the humans…, which, if you've never seen it before is really awesome.

Nevertheless, this chapter is about another thing I hear quite often from people seeking advice for an energetic dog. When I ask them what they do to drain off some of their excess energy I hear, "I take him/her for a long walk/run." Which is great if they know how to walk with the dog but most don't. When I ask if they ever bike ride with the dog the answer is that they don't because they are afraid the dog will pull them down or run into their path and they'll crash. I have never had that experience because I 1) keep them going at a pace where they have to keep moving forward, and 2) I don't give them that much leash – it has to be just enough for space but not too far forward of my legs.

Yet, it started me thinking: If one can walk 5 different energy level dogs at one time with no issues (even passing by other strange dogs), could you bike more than one dog at a time? Capone (Boxer) and Ajax (chocolate Lab) are both great runners and they have a lot of energy so they were great choices for the "experiment". Capone also acted a little bit like a brat when Ajax first came over and had to be corrected twice with a lot of protest. Then they were fine, 3 minutes start to finish. How about riding both of them? And why the bike?

Frankly, I generally have to sprint on my beach cruiser to keep most of the dogs I ride engaged. In my wildest dreams and younger days, there is no way I EVER ran that fast. Not that I am a poor runner. If you have multiple dogs that means multiple rides and yes, sometimes time is a factor. After the first ride you'll probably looking at the hopeful, waiting dog and say, "Gosh, you know, he really doesn't look like he needs a run today." This is, once again, a human inventing what the dog is thinking.

So here is the outcome of the two-dog bike ride. Yes, it can be done with the same principles as one dog. And thanks

to Capone and Ajax, I got the opportunity to do it with them!

Until next time, stay calm and get out on the bike!

Misread Messages - Our Dogs Often Know More Than We Do

L ast weekend, I posted on Facebook that Koa didn't seem to want to stay at the Venice Dog Beach Park and that it was a matter of not reading his "energy" correctly. Some wonderful people read that as he was not feeling well, perhaps even from the heat, and were concerned about his recovery. Koa & I love you guys for the sentiment but it actually made the point of this chapter. If we misread messages and assume we know what we're seeing, then the message is not delivered.

Koa & I had been at the dog beach the previous day and everything was great; we stayed 2 hours and had a fun time. On Sunday, however, he didn't seem to be feeling it. First of all, someone driving their private limo had parked in a very confined area of the parking lot and blocked most of the lot (both coming and going). Their dog, from inside a closed car, was absolutely out of control while the owner sat in the car with apparently no correction. On the way to the entrance, other dogs were barking at the previous one (to correct what pack leader was not) and THEIR owners were not controlling that.

Once inside the grassy dog park area, Koa came in, turned around, and stared at the gate to leave. It took me having to approach him to get him to follow and he was incredibly slow to walk down to where the beach is (about 100 yards). The beach has quite a wide expanse and it was a little crowded, with lots of dog noise in one area so I opted to go further down where it was almost entirely deserted. When I put down my things, Koa was still standing where we had entered the beach area and hadn't moved; again, odd. I went back and had him accompany me to the water, a straighter and closer path than back to the towels. And the energy of the other owners could not have been worse. One particular large dog was humping every dog nearby with all of the owners standing there and laughing that "you can't do that – that's a boy dog!" We walked beyond that, but on the return trip this same dog came out of nowhere and tried humping Koa. Since he was walking behind me I only heard Koa bark and then growl, which still didn't send a message. I went back over to Koa and since Koa had moved the other dog was trying to re-engage. I had to touch correct the other dog and he apparently got the message. No one said anything (lucky for them) because no one was paying attention to a dog that clearly needed management.

Afterward, even though Koa got in the water, it still didn't seem that he wanted to stay. And that's when it hit me: I had misread his message that "this is the wrong energy at

the beach and we shouldn't stay." And he was correct because it was a real aggravation even when we were much farther away. Why had I missed that? Because I was reading the behavior and not the message from Koa's energy.

There are 2 take-aways from this: First, read your dog's

energy and messages they are trying to send without reading into the context of the message, especially when the behavior is vastly different than normal. Second, if you have a dog enforce rules and I mean making rules that are social for humans AND canines. For many reasons, it is NOT okay for a dog to try to hump another dog and can often result in a fight with real injuries to the dogs or the people who will try to jump in. Calm and balanced dogs will never exhibit that behavior because the most dominant one in control is the pack leader. Humans will do the figurative humping with subordinates just to show who is in charge and we all know that is about as unbalanced as they come. Clearly, when Koa returned to the in-law's house, he was happy just to lay in the thick grass away from all of the chaos.

So, until next time, read the message (not the behavior) and enforce (and obey) the rules!

Successes from Failures

ALL of our successes in life come from failures – ours or someone else's. This is a short story about one such failure, and the success that grew out of it.

Mary Bell is a shepherd mix at the Humane Society and rather new. Her card says that she is VERY hard to get out of the kennel and seeing that as a challenge I looked in on her. She is very wary of humans, and would go to the opposite side of the kennel away from any human. I sat in her kennel for about 5 minutes and although she laid down, she never really relaxed. After a hide & seek game several times I decided to close off part of the kennel so I could contain her. After another 10 minutes of sitting – no touch, no talk, no eye contact – she still hadn't truly relaxed so I took a chance on introducing the leash to her.

She was very anxious and was deep into avoidance, but once the leash was on she seemed to snap out of her shell. A short trip to the off-leash yard and she seemed relaxed enough so I took her off the leash. She ran off and stayed at a comfortable distance for quite so time. I wanted to have her be outside and enjoy the fresh air but it seemed as if she was patrolling the perimeter. After I ignored her for a while she got into the pool and laid down.

Success, right? I thought so, until I approached in her direction and she quickly maintained the distance bubble between us. I shadowed her for a while, figuring I would drain some of her energy so she would relax, but Mary Bell is a focused little girl. After about 25 minutes of this dizzying circling she showed signs of being a little more drained, but nowhere close to giving up. I was even beginning to imagine trying to do this in the dark after everyone had gone home... not a pretty picture, but I wasn't going to give up on her.

In the corner is a gated passageway to another yard, also gated. I figured I would open one of the gates and corral her by walking her in that direction. After the third fly by, she entered and I had her. Once again, she was very skittish and thought about snapping at me when I finally reached for her collar. Leash attached, away she went like nothing had happened except for a bit of exercise. The success is that she walks extremely well on the leash. But take the leash off, even in a small kennel, and she shuts down. The solution? Next time, after we're inside, the leash will not come off but rather she can drag it around with her which will make it easier to regain control during the "patrolling".

So what went wrong? I misread that she would do well completely off the leash since she was walking so well on it and forgotten about "testing" this by having her drag the leash on her travels. Just because our own dogs walk well with us doesn't mean that they're ready for that freedom, especially when recall is not their particular strong suit. What we want, and the reality of that happening, is only divided by the investment of time that we put into the outcome and wishing it to happen is, once again, humans rationalizing emotions.

Remember, don't repeat the same failures over and over again while expecting success. Use a different perspective and stay calm and focused!

Gregory DiFranza

Learn about Kobe & Remy!

Kobe & Remy are two pack members of Susan & Dennis that I watched for two weeks. Neither had previously been to the beach or in the water, but as you can see they enjoyed their summer Kamp! These two little guys have a lot of heart, and by the time we had gotten to the second day, they were "running with the big dogs", figuratively and literally. They also would walk on the treadmill to drain some of their energy and swam in the pool – two more things they previously hadn't done.

Don't imagine what your dog CAN'T do, imagine what they CAN and let them impress and surprise you! You'll be a proud pack leader in no time!

What's in a Name?

An old Florida Highway Patrol buddy of mine, Danny Herring, got the chance to become one of the first Canine Troopers, in large part because he was an awesome and very successful drug interdiction trooper. In those days the dogs were all donated pets, and he was teamed with a large Rottweiler. Both did extremely well during the canine academy but the FHP had a problem – the dog's real name was "Lucifer" and they couldn't very well put that on the side of a patrol car.

So they removed the last three letters of the male dog's real name to make "Luci" and Luci and Danny performed very well in the real world. So well that after one particularly huge drug seizure the newspaper ran a front-page story with a large picture of Luci sitting in front of kilos of marijuana with all of his genitalia on display with the caption, "Luci Seizes Marijuana Haul"... which then caused a bit more confusion for everyone, except Luci.

Our dogs don't care about the names we give them, but humans love to put certain labels on their dogs. And sometimes this becomes the story we attach to them, and the energy or mind-set that we exhibit when we are around them, or when humans make excuses for their dogs' (or the owners') behavior. Can you imagine the potential headlines? "Lucifer Captures Drug Runners, Acts as a Warning to Others"... well, duh! Or, better yet, "I don't know why Fluffy just bit you – he never does that!"

All dogs bite, all dogs can be dangerous with the wrong owners, and all dogs are wonderful creatures that are an important step in our histories both personally and as a civilization. But the name is the energy we attach to our dogs, not the other way around. "Koa" is Hawai'ian for Warrior, or Brave. He can be both, and neither. Just as you shouldn't read emotions into dog behavior, don't read energy into our dogs' names. That is merely the personality we attached to them and is HUMAN, not dog. Your dog doesn't "know" your name. He or she only knows what kind of a leader you are, and are not.

Until next time, enjoy your dogs for what they really are – our friends, our companions, and our best buddies. And please show them they have no limitations on how canine they can be!

Welcome Atticus!

Today we welcome Atticus, a one year old Ridgeback buddy of Koa's. We all met several times over the past few months, but after an invitation to walk with our pack he has become a regular. And, as all Ridgeback puppies, a regular clown! As you might guess, Koa hasn't grown out of that, either, and we really hope that they both don't.

Atticus has become a great pack member and wrestling buddy along with MC, whether it's in a hole (claimed by Koa and challenged by Atticus and MC) or the usual "let's run into the water to wrestle away from everyone else" time.

Atticus spent a long weekend with Kamp K-9 Jax Bch and was an awesome close cousin with Koa the whole time. You'll read why he was important to the pack in the coming chapters.

Jameson, the Educator

With the hot "dog days of June" upon us, I thought that instead of just waiting to have another get together/course, I could just share details of some of the things our morning pack is doing and everyone will get some benefit whether you're able to walk with us in the mornings on the beach or not. And thanks to our new friend Jameson, he is able to teach us even when we're absent.

I was a dog handler at the Humane Society and I did it for two main reasons: First, I had the time and I had the knowledge to safely interact with dogs even in an unbalanced environment such as their kennels (THAT is an understatement!). Second, I wanted to help each individual dog with taking away the burden of needing to be in a leadership position all of the time and get a chance to just get outside and be a dog, even for a little bit. It's exhausting for dogs to be in the roles of leaders; but more about that in a minute.

First, the background: Jameson is a mixed breed that two friends have lovingly and graciously volunteered to watch while his owners are away for two weeks on their honeymoon. Jameson, however, apparently hasn't been socialized with other dogs and is very canine/prey driven, which leads to excitement, dominance, and aggression. I don't think he has chosen to do this; dogs who do not have a calm/assertive authority figure think that it is their place to fill that role – it's hardwired into their heredity for survival. That is why they can change so rapidly when animal/dog/breed are respected with calm energy from the pack leader, and the pack leader takes on the responsibility for leadership. It's not in the dog's PRIMARY nature to be a pack leader; they are followers and that's where they are the happiest and most balanced. You can see that in our own pack. However, Jameson thought he had to lead and NO ONE was following him so he had to PROVE that he was the leader, which is very unbalanced and caused his excitement/frustration/dominance and can lead to aggression. U.S. Presidents age significantly when they are in office – that's a clue as to how stressful it is to lead all of the time! And they pitch temper tantrums when no one is listening to them or if everyone wants to follow someone else…. (meet Jameson!).

After several days, Jameson had already improved in the VERY limited time he had been with us, but he was still a challenge. Why? Because he had not had rules/boundaries/or limitations and he protested once he had them, especially since he apparently hasn't had them all of his adult life. So he becomes alert/excited when another dog approaches, and tries to dominate by a lot of noise and "climbing" the other dog (this is "high ground advantage", a tactical term, not "humping" and starts with placing the head on top of the shoulders before climbing with the legs). This is textbook excitement/dominance which leads to aggression and leads to a fight or a bite (human or canine) especially when it's not corrected at the beginning. The key is to prevent, not break up the fight after it starts.

So, timing in a correction is everything. You must have the right type of collar (no harnesses), the right kind of leash (no flexi-leashes) and the collar must be placed correctly (high on the dog's neck just like a dog show) to keep the head up and not down or forward. After the correction, the leash must not have any tension because the dog has to think, "Oh, I get it; they want me to relax." Sound, not name, is used, and never block the dog to get his/her attention (blocking, or standing in front face to face to correct, allows the dog to control human movement – they will always look around your legs, causing you to move back and forth. Too much of that, and the dog may bite to control your movement and get you to stop – his idea of a correction for YOU!). Simply correct, and bring them to YOUR side with both of you facing out – corrections are discipline for unacceptable behaviors, not punishment (so stay calm!).

Remember that this type of correction is a quick tug on the leash followed by relaxing the tension. There is no such thing as, "I have a small dog and his/her neck is too fragile." We are not swinging the dog overhead like a lasso! Small dogs and big dogs alike, their necks are extremely muscular because the skull/nose is in constant movement. Otherwise, just put a whiplash collar on them so their neck won't move at all (and see how happy they are wearing THAT for a while!).

The second morning that correction had to go up a notch for Jameson, after he tried climbing on Koa and got corrected by me. He acted out his protest by trying to climb me after turning at me. Pack leaders are not challenged by followers but if they are, it's not personal. He still didn't know the hierarchy, so to teach that point I put him onto his side in the sand with a couple of seconds of kicking and growling – all just a protest. The follow-through on any correction is important; take the time to do it! He thought that after a couple of seconds he was good to get up on his own... this is just another manifestation of no rules in the past. So after another flip to his other side and being pinned down again until he fully relaxed, he finally surrendered to the exercise and I got up and had him get up AFTERWARDS. I wasn't upset/frustrated/angry/aggressive; I want him to be happy and he will never be a happy dog with that kind of energy or attitude. We are here to help him and the whole thing took less than a minute.

Many people saw the instant transformation that took place in the ANIMAL, DOG part of him afterwards and even though he still needs reminding (that's the BREED part of him remembering the repetitious negative energy in his past), toward the end of the walk he was happy to the point that he invited Koa for play (downward-facing dog position in Yoga is the canine body language of, "Let's play."). This still means that pack leaders have to limit the intensity of the play, just like you should do with your kids, but that behavior change is HUGE in Jameson and has to – and should – take place even for a short while.

All of us have now participated in walking with him (sometimes he is a little challenging in causing us to control the human energy, but that's probably why he is with us) and have walked multiple dogs – including Jameson – side by side with him for a while. His two days I spoke of have translated to only about two hours total! Think about how long it would take to try to rehabilitate a dominant/aggressive human! That is the greatest thing about dogs – with the right energy, they get it, and they get it pretty fast. It only gets easier from there.

One last point: I said earlier that timing is everything in a correction. Last week I had to correct 2 off-leash pits that surrounded Koa on the beach and had switched from greet to pre-attack mode. One understood after I verbally corrected and stepped in, but the other needed the touch. Both understood at that point who the authority figure was and who was in charge and that I wasn't going to let even balanced but very powerful Koa have to defend himself. Afterwards, they walked along with us like the rest of our pack does. The same went for Jameson; he was textbook in face to face initial contact, then the ears went forward with the chest and he moved his head around to the side of their face at the neck – classic pre-attack posture, not smelling the rear. If you wait to correct/touch, you will be too late and the dog will be in control of the fight; too early, and you can initiate the attack from the other dog. Timed well, and you will see the dog flinch to the side and look to see where that just came from, while backing down and they will always look at your eyes, acknowledging that they understand that you mean business. And you should always do this with calm but assertive energy. Most importantly? Once this occurs, start walking and have them follow. This gets them back into the following mode and leaves the incident behind. They'll remember what you want – calm submission, but unlike humans they don't dwell on the incident and neither does the offended dog. And neither should you.

Remember, ALL humans are pack leaders and have the same responsibilities with all dogs, not just a favorite – rules, boundaries, and limitations!

Until next time, stay calm and assertive!

Mahalo to Jameson and Aloha to Suki!

Jameson finished his time with us this morning and was doing great! No matter what, we all always form a connection with dogs we have met and especially the ones we have worked with on THEIR behalf. Jameson seemed happy, proud, and much calmer, walked alongside Koa without as much pulling, and played in the water for a bit. We all wish the best for him in the future – and hope to see him again on the beach real soon! Aloha, our new friend, and mahalo for the opportunity and the trust that you showed us!

So what's next? **Suki**, a Blue Bay Shepherd, will be coming by to meet and greet in two weeks, and staying for about a week in early August. **Cocoa & Ajax**, a Labradoodle and a chocolate lab respectively, have already visited and will be with me for about 4 days in a couple of weeks. More wonderful pups to add to the history of the pack!

Until next time, stay calm & assertive and enjoy your walks with a wonderful creation of God!

Suki!

Suki finally came to stay this week and has been here for a couple of days. Being a wolf hybrid and only a year and a half old, there are some distinct differences. First, she has a large pack at her house (5 in all) so she is socially adept with dogs. However, the wolf part of her dictates that she is a little wary of humans at first, but curious. Once the nose engages and there are no sudden movements, she will warm up after a while. As always, the best human behavior is no touch, no talk, no eye contact and approach sideways with respect; not for the wolf (face it, they're ALL wolves!) but for the animal/dog. Frankly, this is how humans need to introduce themselves to ALL dogs, anyway.

A word about respect: I am the pack leader, but dogs in my control are not my servants, they are my "squad", so to speak. Like a tactical unit, we all have specific strengths and weaknesses and it is my job to figure that out and utilize individuals in my pack to its fullest potential. You cannot do this without respect, and I do not receive respect without giving respect. Human or animal world, it is exactly the same. When I control the pack, I also gain more respect from the dogs in that pack. Why? Because they see that I not only control but protect the pack and that gives them a sense of security and they pay attention to direction even better.

For example, one of the jobs I give Koa is attaching the leash of another dog that needs a leader to his collar. He then follows me, and the other dogs realize what order the pack is in. Koa is perfect for this, but I would not attach another dog to one with issues unless I was certain that the correct message is sent.

During her first day, we immediately went on a pack walk (with Koa, whom she shadows) and later to the beach and into the water, both of which she had not done before. She handled all of it like a regular beach dog and seemed to enjoy the time, since she came back and slept for the next couple of hours.

Suki is also an escape artist. She exited her kennel crate twice within 10 minutes the first night. I heard her walking down the hall to our bedroom to see if everyone was still there. I then devised a system with carabineers that ensures her presence whether she wants it or not... plus, trying to escape an inescapable crate gives her an activity.

Suki's second day of activities ended with a pack bike ride with Lisa and Koa. Suki wants Koa to play with her but he is tolerantly ignoring her because of that unsure energy she still has in new environments. It's getting better, but the pack teaches more about correct behavior than the humans could ever do, and they do it quicker. So on the pack ride, Koa leads the way by showing Suki that we run alongside the bike and not way out into the road. I could keep leash correcting her, but he is much better at the "follow me!" part of being. In fact, when I eventually took both of them so Lisa could video the ride for Suki's owner, she ran even closer to my bike than he ever has, and it helped her immensely.

Since our morning pack walks only last about an hour, Suki has only had about 2 hours of time with new humans. Still, she recognizes them respectfully and has gotten to the point of touching their hands with her nose, a very respectful and trusting behavior.

The next activity: out and around many new people and crowds! Of course, my buddy Koa will be there to show her the way. Until next time, be respectful!

Mahalo, Suki!

T oday we say, "Mahalo!" to Suki for staying at Kamp K-9 Jax Bch and teaching all of us more about dogs and especially about the wolf in all dogs. Thanks to Koa and Atticus, a three-way wrestle-fest took place before

the afternoon pack walk and was a chance for me to observe and have a video record of instinctual play time. You can be sure that if you didn't know anything about dogs it would be quite upsetting and disconcerting to watch – and listen to – how they all play and the interaction of the group.

However, before and after they all seemed as if they have been around each other forever and, in a way, they have – they're all from the *canis* species and they all understand each other. It's only when humans interfere with (and not regulate) the play does it become unbalanced.

A dog in a new environment that shakes, shivers, and tries to jump on their owner is not *afraid*. They are going through a processing of what it is like to be a normal dog instead of what they are used to, and they have a tendency to gravitate to the weakest energy pack leader. Some owners will then pick up their dog, shield them from the perceived "threat", and start telling their dog, "It's okay," in a high-pitched voice. This accomplishes two things: 1) it reinforces the dogs' belief that the energy is weak, and 2)

it shows the other dogs that the handler's energy is weak...
all of which can have instantly devastating effects in the
form of a bite or aggressive tendencies.

I was quite happy to realize that none of the pack was
gravitating to me, they were simply being dogs. This
doesn't mean I didn't have to regulate the intensity, it just
means that aside from regulating intensity I didn't tell
them how to play. Instinctually, they play like they fight or
hunt prey in the animal world. Two Ridgebacks cornering
and chasing a wolf hybrid who is nimbler and faster on the
sprint than they are is a sight to see. Plus, in Suki's case,
she can hold her own against all of them; it's just that they
all never gang up on one unless that one is unbalanced or
has a weak energy. Starting to see a connection now?

Amazingly, Suki would then target Atticus for correction
when he started play fighting with Koa, especially when
Koa wanted to stop. In fact, she was pretty adamant about
it in behavior and sound. Want to know what "assertive"
looks like"? One of my videos shows exactly what message
Suki wanted Atticus to have. And Atticus, being a mostly
balanced one year old, knew it was time to give her what
she wanted... to "knock it off, youngster!"

So, until next time, stay calm, assertive, and let them play! Thanks again, Suki! See you soon!

Cocoa and Ajax Have a Weekend Vacation!

L ast weekend, Cocoa (13-year-old Labradoodle) and Ajax (3-year-old Chocolate Lab) spent a long weekend at Kamp K-9 Jax Bch! Both are sweet dogs, and both had the opportunity to calmly walk with the pack at the beach. Ajax also got to pull me around the neighborhood on the bicycle – and I say "got to" because he pulled me at top speed for well over a mile in the middle of a driving rain storm, and still wanted to keep going!

Both have a different energy but when together with Koa, and my son's dog, Kye, everybody had the right kind of energy for whatever activity we were all doing. In fact, Cocoa would lead the pack quite often on the beach walks and was always up for any activity, whether it was walking or just lying on the sand watching the "youngsters" wrestle around. We hope to see them both again soon!

News from Around the Dog World!

O kay, so it's been a little while since I've written and there have been tons of dogs – and their humans – saved! I also just graduated two more Canine Leadership classes and two Dog Park Behavior classes in addition to more than 40 individual sessions in the past month alone! And, I have to admit, there have been some amazing transformations in the humans. I know the dogs will get it but convincing humans to stop living in the past is the harder part and I'm proud to report that no one in the past 4 months has given up on their dog! In fact, many of the Pack Leaders-in-training have pushed themselves beyond where they were in the beginning! In spite of other "trainers" they've hired....

I say this because my clients have told me some horror stories about what they have been told about their dogs and themselves by people who pass themselves off as dog trainers and don't know the first thing about dog psychology. I'll say this: If you don't know dogs or dog psychology be honest with yourself and with the person who needs help and is doing what is best for their dogs: admit it up front. That's why those same "treat trainers" have a disclaimer on their websites that states they reserve the right to decline to work with any dog. The disclaimer itself is unnecessary! Just say, "This is out of my league or abilities."

It's ridiculous, dangerous and irresponsible to tell clients to, "Shut up," (yes, this happened), or that one client's two dogs are so aggressive with each other that they need to be euthanized without ever leashing them up and walking them (again, this happened and was told to me by my client as I sat on the floor with both dogs together after working with them for less than 20 minutes apiece), or that they will need many sessions for hundreds of dollars with these "trainers" who try to use treats and snacks as a distraction for a dog that, at that time, is in a Red Zone. Affection during an unstable state of mind tells me they know ABSOLUTELY NOTHING about dog psychology or pack mentality.

I understand that there are different levels of expertise in any endeavor and there is a place for obedience trainers who use treats with dogs that are in the correct state of mind. But this is not a "one size fits all" occupation. If your dogs does well with treats then please use that. But if they don't, the next option is not to kill them because the so-called "trainer" can't work with them!

This is not a new rant for me; you've read and heard me say to be wary of people who say they're trainers yet don't use instinctual communication with dogs and instead use the bark in their face/throw down cans of coins/use treats/"shock collars for everyone"/etc. approaches toward training. Hey, they have great marketing histories, but do they have successes beyond what their websites exclaim?

On to something different! During the past few months I have made several presentations to different groups

Congratulations, Pack Leaders!

statewide that foster or rescue dogs and have been honored to make these talks to great pack leaders who really want to learn more about the dogs that come into their lives. I have been able to work with unknown dogs that were volunteered by their owners, and they have been able to see the reality of what I talk about. I will be working with some folks in south Florida with dog aggressive dogs and, as usual, Koa will be my wing-dog as he has been on numerous occasions and always with a successful result. Koa is a great teacher and I have learned a lot from him!

Go walk your dog and be social, and don't avoid situations but embrace them as a learning experience for you! Our dogs are our teachers and some of our teachers are harder on us to improve and expect more out of us than others! Until the next time, stay calm and smart!

The Falconer's Apprentice

A hh, the look of the wild dog, presented by the Dog Falconer... or a welder (I'm obviously trying to make this subject nobler than it actually is!). I took this photo in the UAE a couple of years ago, during an exhibition on Falconing at the Al Ain Zoo, and another one of Louie, one of our friends' dogs (no, Louie did NOT go with me!). The reason this came to mind was a story related to me recently by a client who had a "dog trainer from a major company" come out to help with her puppy. So what's the problem, you ask? The puppy was not what dog the "trainer" kept focusing on. It was the other small dog similar to old Louie here... in fact, at 13 the dog was much older than 10 year old Louie.

Once again, here's a client who tells me that a so-called dog trainer told her the dog is aggressive and therefore showed up with a falconers/welders glove (forearm length leather) and suggested she buy one "that you can get down at the hardware store" so he won't bite her (by the way, not a problem that she encountered). Numerous times on numerous days, this owner reminded him that he was not there for the dog that is old, grumpy, and very manageable. Still, this person – with a "sorcerer's apprentice" in tow – continued to poke at the little guy's face in an effort to get him to bite the glove. Why? "So that he can learn that biting isn't going to make me back away." After that didn't work to his satisfaction, he suggested an e-collar for the 10 pound guy.

She paid a lot of money for this, and told him not to come back (I'll bet he won't put THAT on his testimonials page). She also said that her little guy REALLY didn't like him at all, on three visits to her house for the other dog. Why am I relating this to you? She told me this while I am petting her "monster falcon" and he's curled up on the floor next to me. Can you say, "EGO PROBLEM" and dog illiterate? By the way, did this little guy bark at me and posture when I came in? You bet he did, but I'm not the other guy, either.

Just as I would not go into the restaurant business because I once ate at a restaurant, owners who want their money's worth when they might be at their wit's end and feeling hopeless with their dog might want to do a little digging into what a person's background in dealing with dogs REALLY is. Don't just read the marketing. There are many YouTube videos and segments of Cesar Millan available and just because they're watched doesn't make one a "dog expert" simply by deciding to change professions on a whim. It is similar to someone looking at YOUR job position and deciding, "I can do that," with no experience or well-placed dedication.

Please don't mistake this as a commercial for me – there are many different methods and, as we tell our tactical officers during training, "It's not THE way, it's A way." However, just as in tactical training, there is a lot riding on the fact that people are going to pay for and then use what you teach them and it has to fit that individual or process. If not, for dog/people training anyway, it could mean the end of the dog's life, or a shelter existence which may mean the same thing.

The mantra is the same as always: it's not about you, it's about the dog. So, until next time, stay calm, take the emotions out of dealing with your dog, and do your homework when selecting a professional!

The Piper Needs to Pay Koa!!

K amp K-9 Jax Bch has been busier than ever! But I would like to share two notable events with you. The first is Lucy, a Great Dane/Lab mix who has energy issues; this means that she doesn't get her entire energy reserve depleted and this can result in anxiety or becoming way too mischievous in her effort to burn off the excess energy.

I bike rode her back to the house and then decided to put her on the treadmill – her first time. It took her less than 30 seconds to get the idea that the ground was moving and that she had to concentrate on propelling herself forward, and she did quite well. During the taping, which I did to show Lucy's owner that she would do it since she was considering buying a treadmill for those occasions, two other dogs named Piper and Brandi were with us at Kamp

K-9 Jax Bch. Of course Koa was there and I had all of the dogs in the Florida Room to create a little distraction so Lucy would work through the challenge.

While editing the video, I noticed something I had not previously seen on the tape and certainly didn't see when it happened: Koa intentionally and subtly moved Piper out of the way from in front of the treadmill, which is a dangerous place to be since the dog may move forward and through the front to get off if they are suddenly distracted – which actually happened one minute later. When you watch the video, I slowed it down during that time so you can see it in action. And you could see that it was a pack leader behavior on Koa's part since I was unable to see it. I'm not saying that he knew it was going to happen, but he's been there enough to know that's not where you want to be when something happens.

And, a week later, another dog named Lola, got on the treadmill for her first time and inside 20 seconds was walking on the treadmill without the leash attached for a total of almost an hour! When I sent that video to her owner, she thought that I had doctored the tape somehow (but I'm not that good!). Just remember that if you are working with your dog on a treadmill, the introduction has to be calm, assertive, and supportive of the end result – one that has your dog being mentally challenged AND successful in that challenge, which only improves your status in the dog psychology aspect of their life.

Until next time, challenge your pack to become better – that's what a true pack leader does!

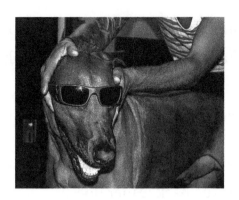

Balanced Koa

Cesar Millan uses his balanced pack to do things that we, as humans, cannot do. It's a great idea and it truly works, as long as the dog is balanced and you stay patient. I have used Koa in this way many times and I must admit it is mind-boggling how easy it is and how fast it works.

One morning, Jameson was still a little into the pulling mode on the pack walk and while I was walking both he and Koa side by side (with Koa on the outside), Koa's leash started hanging in front of Jameson's neck. He immediately INSTANTLY switched to walking like a real dog, absolutely no tension on the leash and no pulling, controlling his own pace to match Koa's pace.

As often as I have used Koa by connecting another dog's leash to his (like Kobe & Remy, and other dogs that need a little help from another dog), I could have slapped myself for not thinking of this. Why? Because, as humans, we make things so complicated when the real challenge is to make things simple. Our entire pack – Elvis, MC, Koa, Abby, and Capone – do this when they are together but it is always so amazing to watch it unfold... and you must pay attention because it happens so fast!

Also this morning, after the pack walk, Koa and I went back down to the water just to cool off. There at the water's edge was an older woman trying to control and highly energetic Lab/Dane mix. It was painful to watch. The dog (on a harness, of course!) was pulling, jumping, lunging, grabbing the leash and pulling the owner off balance right & left with it. They were generally travelling in our direction (well, the dog was; the owner was following!) and it was one of those things that you can't stop watching...

When they got closer, I asked how old the puppy was and she told me he was 2 years old, a rescue, and had not learned how to walk after 2 months with her. I also commented that he certainly has a lot of excess energy and that he truly had control of that harness. Her belief was that he was so much better with the harness on as compared to a collar and she can control him with the harness. I just could not say anything to that; if I only had a video of the previous 5 minutes to show her it still might not have done any good. Of course, during this time Koa is standing with me and just looking at the dog in his calm way and the dog just stood still and then very respectfully started licking Koa's ears (huge sign of respect in the dog world) and calmed way down.

Koa didn't start off as perfect and he has had his times (Lisa & I used to call him our 98 percenter – 98% of the time he was great, but the other 2% he ignored our direction and went his own way). However, adulthood and lots of reinforcement with patience is an absolute investment in your dog.

Stay patient and assertive!

Kye

Kye is my son Ben's dog and he is a chow mix with a lot of energy, especially since he's just now 6 months old. Kye folds into any pack very easily since he has a playful spirit that is boundless! After meeting Ziva (a chocolate lab) on the beach, he ran with her into the waves chasing a weighted decoy for 30 minutes AFTER already walking the usual distance (about 2 miles).

And then he slept most of the day... so hard that he peed in his sleep, and he is really good at going outside and not having accidents. You just gotta give a pass on that; we've all been that tired before...

Toby, the Bionic Shepherd

Toby, Bob & Marie's wonderful German Shepherd, stayed at Kamp K-9 Jax Bch for a short while and had a great time while his pack leaders were visiting family. A wonderful, balanced addition to the walk. After their return, Toby hurt his leg while chasing a ball, or a squirrel, or a bird, or whatever caught his fancy. X-rays determined that he had a torn meniscus on one leg, and hip dysplasia on the other side. So Toby is now sporting a metal plate and screws on the injured leg with a very good prognosis (if he can let it heal). Does this mean he'll sink the next time he goes in the water?

Good Luck, Toby – we're rooting for you, buddy!

Three More Success Stories!

Kamp K-9 Jax Bch has been busy the past couple of weeks! Three more success stories in Leo, Herman, and Luci!

First, Leo: Leo had a great time on the morning beach walk and walked with the pack very well. However, Leo has been known to gulp/inhale his food, or anyone else's food that might be nearby (I lost a hamburger, wrapper and all, when I turned my back… but I'm over it… sort of). So I decided to see if he could control himself. After having him lay down, I took a piece of cheese (the "Good Stuff": Kraft white American cheese, no less) and gave him a small piece. Then I put the rest on a plate and had him wait, which he did. I moved it closer and he thought about it but only looked while he licked his chops. I moved it even closer and turned my head and body and out of the corner of my eye I could see him bending down to the plate with his head turned sideways so he could keep an eye on me! I voice-corrected him and he stopped with a look like, "I wasn't going to eat that!" I moved it under his head and we both sat there for 3 minutes; he never looked at it – in fact, he tried to look everywhere BUT the cheese. Then, of course, I let him get the cheese. Job well done, Leo!

Next up, Happy Herman. Herman is the kind of dog that comes into a room and knows how to introduce himself in a calm but happy way to everyone. He got to swim in the ocean with the big dogs, swam at the dog park all the way

across the lake, and participated in a spaghetti dinner hosted by Dan, one of the morning pack leaders, and all of our dogs. Look out, Tim (Herman's owner): tons of people wanted to take Herman home – he is the consummate balanced pack member!

Last is Luci. Two-year-old Luci is a bundle of energy that loves to jump to say hello and was not super great on the walk. Her owner enlisted my help and we met on the

beach with my balanced Koa. Luci had some energy to off-load (which she accomplished by digging holes while we talked) but after a short discussion on some basics with the owner, we started working together on changing the leash, rules/boundaries/limitations, and the correct pack leader attitude. Rehabilitating a dog is a process and the process progresses much quicker when the human is on board, which she really was! After the beach we went to the dog park to let her drain the rest of the physical energy after the mental exertion, and to observe and learn how dogs interact. When dogs exhibit an unbalanced energy other dogs will correct that and a Doberman named Jago did just exactly that with her when she was playing too excitedly with Koa. Dogs can make that correction faster and with long-lasting effects than humans and it worked beautifully!

I'm happy to report that this morning we met Luci and her owner on the beach and the difference was night and day! The walk was relaxed and you could tell that Luci's owner has put the work in even during the short time we were together. She looked every bit the part of a true pack leader! She also shared a photo of Luci after the session: lying on her back, feet in the air, eyes wide open but sound asleep! Way to go!

Until the next time, stick to the basics, be calm, and enjoy the time with your dog!

The Second-Best Thing About Working with Dogs

During this spring/summer I've had a lot of client visits and many of them will ask, "You must really love what you do, working with dogs." The truth is that I do, even more than I like working with police

officers from all over the world. But during a client visit out of town, I began thinking about that statement while I was driving but it wasn't until I was taking an assessment walk with their dog that it dawned on me – I love what I do, but why? This is actually a two-part answer. The first answer is that the best thing about helping people with their dogs is that the dogs are happier and in a healthier state of mind. When they finish with the session they are smiling and less stressed, they are calm & relaxed, and I often hear, "I've never seen them like that before." And the dog's state of mind is really important but I always say that I knew the dog could do it, I'm really there to help the human with canine leadership.

The second-best thing about working with dogs is that I get to help the humans. It occurred to me that when I am working with the canines I snap a photo showing them in their element; calm walking, smiling, happy, snoozing

after the session or a picture with their owners walking them with a loose leash. It's that last element there that began my thought – why aren't I taking before and after pictures of the owners' faces?

The simple answer is that I don't wish to put them on the spot when they're not in the best frame of mind. Their reality is that their dog(s) are misbehaving and they are at

the end of their rope because they don't know what to do to fix it. Their faces are strained and drawn and they often are frustrated with the whole thing and half of the time they call me as a last resort (either because other training didn't work for them or that are on the verge of having their dog removed and euthanized). That's a lot of stress!

The most amazing transformation takes place in the humans (remember that the dogs could ALWAYS do what is expected) toward the end of the session when they are able to not only walk their dog with a loose leash but to also better manage behaviors in other areas of their lives. THAT'S where the "before & after" pictures would really be remarkable. Calm, confident humans walking their dogs. Controlling unwanted behaviors with less stress. And a relaxed countenance while having FUN! Which is what walking with another being should be.

Practice walking with leadership for the dog's sake. They are happier and have a healthier state of mind when they are where they belong in the pack because they are not

confused, tense, or frustrated with their human counterparts. Be a teammate with your dog, but be a team leader. Tactically speaking, a team leader will dictate what the team does and circumvents or changes poor decisions made by team members. Our dogs should have self-control over themselves and as such will be easier to manage. But if you aren't leading then you are a follower.

Why do I take the picture at the end? I want the humans

to have a different reality and I post it on social media so their friends and family also have a different reality. Am I going to take pictures at the beginning? No, that would serve no real purpose because what we want is change and moving forward, not a comparison of what the past represented and staying there; that's what got us to the problems in the first place.

Until next time, stay calm and keep moving forward!

Shopping with your Pack

Koa and I recently went to the St. John's Town Center in Jacksonville, FL to shop for one small item, but I'm always looking for an opportunity to challenge him a little more. So a nice, long walk around the stores and traffic, people and other dogs, is a good idea. Plus, the long walk around doesn't seem that long when you're walking with your pack member. Unless it's with Koa, and then people want to stop and talk or pet him... again, not a chore but also not something you can do on a time frame. Take your time and live in the moment...

Earlier, I had taken Koa into the bank with me, at a branch I haven't taken him to in the past. The manager (whom I know) was taken aback by his size and was genuinely concerned for a fleeting moment to know if he was a good guy or if he was one of the ones I rehabilitate. I told her that even if it was, I would never bring a dog that needed that much direction into a business. At the time, I thought it strange but then I passed it off as unfamiliarity. Until later...

Koa and I walked around "downtown Town Center", over a Koi bridge, and back toward the courtyard outside of restaurants all the while watching people do one of three things when they passed him: smile, act concerned and avoid him (he always could not care less while we're walking), or flee in terror. Yes, as if he were a character at Universal Studio's Halloween Horror Nights looming behind them and carrying a chainsaw (heeeey.... no, don't give me any ideas!). Which is not only amusing to me but also to the large number of people who also see that and think it's hilarious... which it is!

But after we went into several stores and got what I was looking for, we drove over to PetSmart just to walk around because we were already there. And then it got more interesting. I've learned to read most dog handler's energy from a distance by how they walk or interact with their dog while they're in the pet shops. And a couple of ladies and their behavior caught my eye in there before I even knew what kind or if they had a dog. I call this behavior "short-stepping" because these handlers take really small steps around or with their dogs because they don't want to be caught off-guard and fall WHEN the dog pulls them. They walk around their dog instead of having the dog give them respectful space, and the dog is ALWAYS ahead of them while they short-step to keep up; in other words, the dog is totally in control of everything. And while it seemed a little disturbing at first, it got even worse.

The dog was a very large Doberman Pinscher and was absolutely the pack leader; neither woman was controlling his state of mind. A couple with a Siberian Husky walked in through the door and it took ITS handler over toward the Doberman with now both of them dictating the introduction. And it went exactly as it always does with weak leaders. Both got extremely aggressive and the Husky's handler was a little less tense/anxious than the Doberman's handler so the Husky was at least easier to control. The Doberman's handlers both got nervous, fearful, and stayed weak by trying to muscle the dog back while saying, "It's okay, it's okay." Which it most certainly was not. Since Koa and I were a distance away (again, Koa couldn't care less) we decided to walk to the other side of the store all the while listening to the handlers shouting, toenails scraping, and employees telling them they would open another lane just so that these folks could check out quicker.

So when people are unsure of a dog is it misplaced fear and borderline cynophobia? Or do they have a well-founded concern? Real pack leaders such as us don't like to admit it, but in reality these folks have a well-founded belief because there ARE that many unbalanced handlers in this world. Not unbalanced as in, "Hey, you can't control your dog," (that possibility ALWAYS exists), but unbalanced as in they thought it would be a grand idea to bring a dog they cannot control at all into a business. And when dogs aren't allowed in some stores this is the reason why.

What's the moral of this story? Continue to challenge your dog and yourself to be the best, most balanced and calm leaders you can be. Yes, your dog can be a leader also; even leaders have to follow someone else. Your dog should be the one people say, "That dog is the reason we want dogs in here," not the reason they put the "service animals only" sign out.

Lisa, Koa and I are going to the Gulf Coast area next week to visit family and work with some aggressive dogs in South Florida. Oh, and go to a Dog Beach and walk around the mall and shop with him, of course. Until the next time, stay calm and be the role model for future dog handlers!

I Got to Be a Dog!

I've got some great stuff coming up to share with you guys, but before I put those stories together with time to do them justice, I HAD to share that I got the chance to be a dog for part of a day! While helping the Jacksonville Humane Society with dog handling at a mini-adoption event I got asked if I was willing to jump into the bulldog mascot suit and wave at people and wander around the event.... um, YES! This awesome event was hosted by a car dealership on their day off and they were wonderful, helpful hosts who also fed everyone for free! Plus, with the little play on words on the sign and kids in cars wanting to high five the dog, who wouldn't want to do it?

Was it hot? Yes! Was it fun! Absolutely! And getting adoration from (almost) everyone can be addictive – I can see why dogs (and many celebrities) can get unbalanced very quickly. Which should serve as a reminder to us to reward the acceptable state of mind, not the immediate behavior. It might work if we did that with misbehaving celebrities.... hmmm....

Fun Times Ahead!

I t's Halloween and holiday seasons are coming up soon! Are you and the pooches ready for it? Festive times usually mean visitors: friends, new acquaintances, family. How does your dog respond to this?

I hope that you have done some work throughout the year on calm approaches to doorbells and the inherent excitement that visitors bring. Here are a couple of quick tips to make your upcoming festivities less stressful!

1. Do some training exercises before the big day. Doorbells and knocks on the door are an instant stimulus for a lot of dogs. Someone arriving at your house does not mean out of control behavior, no matter what size of dog you have.

2. Stay calm even when YOU are excited to see your guests. Your dog feeds off your energy.

3. Putting the dog in another room never allows either of you to work through the things you want changed. Be firm, and remember that after the guests leave, your furry friend is still with you ready to do what you want them to do. Give them direction!

4. If your dog is still a work in progress, advise your guests to do three simple things (and this is hard to do for humans): No touch, no talk, no eye contact until calm submission is demonstrated.

5. Jumping dogs are probably the most common complaint. Do not (and don't have your guests) back away from the dog or lean over the dog. These behaviors by humans invite a jump. If you have a visitor who is a bit more frail, claim the space and require your dog to be calm and give space. If the dog jumps, walk into the dog and be firm about following through. You want your dog to give everyone respectable space so require that before you turn away. Remember: the less sound, the better.

6. Hopefully you have worked on food or candy grabbing behaviors. Remember that many dogs can

be adversely affected by eating chocolate and other food items. If you haven't done the work in advance, keep treats out of reach and make sure that your dog has something healthy to snack on and keep them busy.

7. And last, have fun and stop worrying or micromanaging your dog. EXPECT wanted behaviors and your dog has a greater chance of succeeding. Expect unwanted behaviors, and your dog will still succeed in bringing you your wish!

Until next time, have fun with friends, family, and newcomers as well as your dog!

Happy Thanksgiving!

T his is just a quick reminder chapter today concerning Thanksgiving. First, I want to tell you how thankful I am that many of you are Kamp K-9 Jax Bch clients and that ALL of you read the adventures of the pooches that we all come across! Thank you from your dog, also, for the effort and love that you show them every day, even on the trying days!

Thanksgiving means friends, families, visitors, food, and excitement. Remember that with all of the temptations that our canine family members have with new scents and people, it's important to stay calm and relaxed if you want a calm and relaxed dog. Remember the No Touch, No Talk, No Eye Contact rule and please pass that along to your guests, until the right state of mind returns (calm and submissive). If your dog hasn't had the benefit of working through the problems of excitement or aggression in advance (hint: Christmas is coming soon), you should practice that three-item rule consistently. Love them, but loving them at the right time makes things so much easier for everyone, including our dogs. Don't give affection or the, "Now, calm down, Pookie, it's all right, baby," unless you just WANT that unwanted behavior repeated over and over.

Also, remember that just like in the movie, "A Christmas Story" and the neighbor Bumpkiss' hound dogs, they love turkey just as much as any other family member so be a little more vigilant. Especially with our food-grabbing buddies out there (watch the four-legged ones, also!).

It's such a temptation to include our dogs in the goodies at mealtime, but doing this at the table will encourage the same behavior on the day after Thanksgiving, and every other day. It's an investment in your future... just put it in their bowl and they will enjoy it just the same. There are some foods which are toxic or dangerous to dogs that we know are delicious for us. Use common sense and a little bit of giblets in their food. Leave out the cranberries, anything with onions, and especially no turkey legs to gnaw!

Lastly, remember the daily rituals of exercise, discipline, and affection. A dog with much of the energy drained listens and behaves so much better. Take the time to take them for a long walk, a run, or even a trip to the dog park before the big event (it will do YOU good, too!). During the eating and fellowship time with your guests, remember that your dog still has their routine (especially bathroom breaks) and you'll need to remember their ritual or else they will remind you during dinner in a most inconvenient way, especially because of the excitement.

Have a Happy, Calm and Safe Thanksgiving to you and yours, and give your canine companion a hug for me!

First Coast Living Goes to the Dogs with Kamp K-9 Jax Bch on Live TV!

Set your DVR's for Thursday, September 10, 2015 at 11 a.m. (repeat at 2 p.m.) for Kamp K-9 Jax Bch and the pack LIVE on First Coast Living, WTLV-12! The pack (Koa, along with Faith and Redford) will be appearing and sharing information on being balanced and calm. This will be the first time in front of cameras in a studio for the dogs, so I'm excited to see how all of that will go for them!

In the past several weeks I have had the pleasure of continuing to stay busy, helping to bring out the pack leader in dog owners and helping dogs to become the dog they need to be. If there is one thing that has become absolutely clear, it is that when dogs follow a ritual of calm, assertive leadership we get the calm, submissive dogs we want. The problem is that sometimes we want things to happen without any (or little) effort on our part. I've said this before: the work you put into your leadership skills with your dogs will give you a huge return.

But when I say "work", it doesn't mean it has to be a chore! Changing our focus and looking to challenge ourselves as well as our dogs is incredibly rewarding when you get to improve yourself as much as the dog. Having a household with less stress, less constant noise, less frustration makes the human healthier and happier. And you know that it makes our dogs healthier and happier as well.

I suggest that you use the percentage system of reviewing your day with your dogs. I cannot tell you how many times, at the end of Lisa's and my day with a younger Koa, we would admit, "Today he was a 90%'er." That means he did great, but he – or we – needed improvement in some areas. It also means that every day that percentage would change; sometimes up, sometimes down. But it would keep us focused on the results down the road rather than results in the moment. Now, I think most days Koa is a 1000%'er. Most days. Meaning with dogs, as in humans, every day is different and can have a different outcome.

But, like with humans, if we dwell on the past we are destined to be unprepared for the future.

Until next time, continue to follow the pack on Facebook and Instagram, and stay calm and be a 100%'er for your pack!

Meet the Most Dominant Dog I've EVER Met!

I was recently asked by a new friend to help his friends that have an aggressive dog. This person, who has military and current handling experience, was perplexed by how incredibly aggressive this dog was when he tried to help. The dog is about 2 years old and is being fostered (and hopefully eventually adopted by a forever owner) by a family that already have 4 other dogs and with one exception are all small breeds. This guy, Hamilton, was purported to be super human aggressive and the caller had already tried to help with this guy by being introduced and hopefully taking him on a walk. Apparently, this turned out disastrous as he was attacked and bitten several times and his description to me was, "I tried to take him

214

on a walk but he was hanging off of my pant leg the whole time."

Now, while that might sound a bit humorous (this guy is bigger than me) it conjures a different picture if you start thinking about how to break that dangerous cycle of behavior. Adding to the misconception of some people is that fact that Hamilton is a Papillion, weighing in at about 9 pounds! So from that description (and kind of a challenge in a "we'll see what happens when YOU try doing this" kind of way) I agreed to meet with the family and their friend who wanted to see the whole thing and how it might be done.

(A word of caution: when working with an aggressive dog, every dog is different and every situation has to be assessed without the story that comes with the dog becoming the reality because that is where mistakes are made. With aggressive dogs a mistake means you or someone else getting bitten. All techniques or training plans differ, also, dependent upon what the dog is showing at the time. One size does not fit all.)

My suggestion was to have the dog either outside or confined somewhere in the house at first because the family did not know how to control the aggression and would just let it happen when new people came to the house. That way, we could talk about how and why things happen and the introduction beyond that would be more controlled and less stressful for everyone involved. When I arrived the dog was outside and barking at the fence while the foster mom and I spoke briefly outside. She asked if I would like to come in and meet the rest of the family and we went into the house.

The problem was that none of the dogs were confined, including Hamilton, and all rushed the door when I came in. To be fair, all the others, while loud, were relatively respectful… except Hamilton. Hamilton rushed through everyone else at breakneck speed in an extremely aggressive manner (bared teeth and maintaining EYE CONTACT with me), latched onto my leg and began humping it furiously while keeping that eye contact and snapping his jaws. Had it not been so disrespectful in a pack world it would have been hilarious. But that type of behavior is absolute red zone aggressive and over the top dominant and in the real pack world would have resulted in his immediate death.

One hard corrective touch later and now he was in full blown aggression because his challenge was met with rules and this little guy hasn't had any, because of his back story and his lack of socialization. His target, while he still went after my shoes and legs, was still my face even from so far down. So the ritual of staying calm and claiming his space little by little began, and this included having to block his rushes with my foot and leg. At one point I offered my shoe for him to go after, and when he did he got to find out that he could not get the outcome he was looking for – the shoe didn't back away, in fact the shoe kept advancing. This actually went on for several minutes where I had to back him all the way down the hall and into the living room. I then asked the foster mom to put my leash on him because between the 4 other dogs and 5 extra people (and the fact I wanted to start the whole introduction with him on a leash to begin with), it was not going to progress without me changing his environment right away. She put on the leash and when she passed it to me Hamilton didn't like having a slip lead on at all (Why? Because a slip lead controls the focus of the dog and you can more directly influence state of mind instead of the harness he usually wears… even by their admission, he will do this when walking and when he comes across people he will act the same way until he's picked up by the harness and placed in another location).

My handler friend had already expressed concern with "damaging the throats of small dogs" by using a slip lead. I assured him that when placed correctly and using the self-control the pack leader is supposed to use in correcting, the risk is significantly reduced, especially since you should not be swinging the dog like a lasso, anyway.

Hamilton stopped his temper tantrum (because he was now REALLY tired) in about 15 seconds of realizing, "Oh, maybe this isn't working," and then I explained to everyone what was next. Completely out of the regular order of things the door exercise and the walk were going to be first. I heard my friend say, "Well, here we go!" because HIS attacks kept going at this point (by the way, different intro, different leash system, didn't wait for submission and calm before the next step). But at this point, I knew the outcome because real pack leaders live in the moment.

I walked to the front door, reminded Hamilton to wait, opened the door, stood for a second or 2, then walked out the door and into the yard, Hamilton walking just behind with a loose leash. I heard from behind me, "He was hanging off my pants at this point before," which I reminded him that this introduction and leadership is different. The ritual had changed and the dog changed with it. The walk continued with my friend walking behind.

Two things at that point needed to change immediately. One, is that Hamilton was showing on the walk that he is a back of the pack guy, way too nervous and anxious for that previous behavior to be natural (aggression is a result of tension and his tension was a back of the pack guy thrusting – literally! – himself to the front of the pack and setting rules which even he couldn't follow). Meaning, he has to be following. Second, my friend's reality was that he was attacked viciously by Hamilton and that it was going to happen again. So we had to walk as a pack. To have a nice transition, Hamilton was on my left and my friend was on the right and he even remarked that it looked like Hamilton was enjoying this. I agreed and switched Hamilton to my right side, placing him in between both of us and while he was a little unsure, the dog left that behind after 20 feet. The rest of the walk was uneventful, including coming across other people and dogs and having him walk Hamilton most of the way back to the house.

Arriving back at the house, I knew the real work was about to begin with the family but I enlisted the aid of two pack leaders in training, the son and daughter. Doing the doorbell exercise, teaching the correct timing of the corrections and doing it all in a more calm and assertive way, these 2 blew most adults I work with out of the water with how attentive, proficient and committed they were to the whole process. The walk was no different with both of them preforming outstandingly (assertive, loose leash, calm) with their respective dogs all the while doing it in front of a neighbor's house with a strange dog laying in the front yard.

To end the session, I suggested they each walk 2 dogs at a time, something they never considered doing by their reaction because neither dog had been good on the walk before. I showed them that it could be done and then handed over the leashes to the son, who wanted to go first anyway. And it was a beautiful sight to see when both of them took leashes in hand and became true pack leaders immediately.

Does this "fix" Hamilton? Not by a long shot. He needs to be rehabilitated and socialized and his behavior is not uncommon for this breed when not socialized. But now they have the tools to move forward, along with the rest of the pack. Whether they keep Hamilton or not, they have the tools to help him get corrected and social, but now the work really starts and it can get hard. Staying consistent and calm/assertive changes a dog's behavior and state of mind and should become the new reality for the humans in their lives. The rest of the challenges that lie ahead should be fun for everyone.

Until the next time, stay calm/assertive and have fun challenging yourself and your dog!

Having Faith in Faith

Faith the Airedale came to Kamp K-9 Jax Bch yesterday under the cloud of being fairly dog aggressive and reactive. I know, because I've seen it firsthand, even with Koa. Since she will be here for 10 days I decided that the strategy would be strict rituals, including Faith being dropped off by her owner and from the car going straight into a long walk. I picked some wooded areas for her so that she would start engaging her nose, some swamp areas, and generally anything that is different from what she is used to. The walk went well, and upon our return the bike came out and we went on a short energy-draining ride.

Meeting the other pack at the house was next. Koa was already familiar to her but I had another dog, "Piper" (not the previous Piper) who is a Briard (an ancient French breed developed as sheepdogs) who is young and not completely social yet, either. So, Faith had a muzzle for the short duration (which was important that she have) and had to go into a relaxed and calm state. Faith will get calm, but not relaxed and I knew that was the challenge with the meeting. After the intense introduction, Faith was put on her side and I waited for her to relax, which took several minutes. Afterwards, the muzzle was off and while you still have to monitor behavior, you have to let the dogs sort it out. Corrections cannot come if you don't let the dogs make their mistakes, and staying calm is the Pack Leaders' first order of business. After a few short corrections, everyone was getting along.

Faith did go after Shaka, the cat, and actually barely got her mouth on him before I could touch correct. No aggression toward any animal or human is ever allowed and after two severe corrections, Shaka eventually could walk past Faith and Faith would pay him no mind. Calm states of mind for corrections are the key, even if the corrections are intense. Remember, the corrections have to match the intensity of the behavior you want corrected.

Feeding rituals are just that – rituals that can be expected by dogs without a lot of change. Mornings are runs (bikes or otherwise), potty breaks at the house, food (calm state of mind for all before the food goes down and all food can be picked up and handled by humans even while eating without displaying a negative response), back outside for potty breaks, and play time if necessary. In less than 12 hours, Faith actively invited both Koa and Piper to play. Koa, being more balanced, was all about the "calm down first" part, as Faith still didn't have a long history of calm play, but she learned quickly.

Piper does not have the ability, being young, to calm down quite so quickly and was having problems not being skittish around Faith. A sprinting bike ride later, and a small explosion where Piper went after Faith and then bounced me with her head when I initially corrected that behavior. She needed to be put on her side to relax, and then the fun began.

Here is where the most important part of being in control of EVERYTHING for the Pack Leader is important. Koa has learned that when I have to go into a more intense leadership position correct a dog at the house, he does not have to help me. He knows I have it. And by helping, I mean that other members of the pack will try to bite-correct (even though there are those that will say "that

NEVER happens in the real dog world") the offending dog to help the pack leader. In another chapter I told you that instability, a.k.a. aggression especially directed at Pack Leadership, is an offense that in the survival world will mean death to the offending party whether it be by ostracizing or immediate execution. Immediate because the continued survival of the pack depends upon balance and a cohesive direction for the social order.

Faith did not know this part yet and while correcting Piper, Faith wanted to help me by charging in. This was not a response to the initial problem Piper had with Faith – Faith had already backed off on her own without being told while I began to deal with Piper. Koa, on the other hand, never stopped chewing a piece of mulch (see? Balance...). While backing Faith off, Piper felt the need to defend herself (it wasn't necessary, but she didn't know that yet) and wound up catching my hand in her snap at Faith. In face of being bitten (twice for me in the last month, both times unintentional on the dog's part and both times on the same hand) you have to remain calm, assertive, and not affected by the explosion because THAT is viewed as weakness by the pack, also. Your response – staying calm and unaffected by the incident – also shows the pack that you are in control, and a true calm leader;

and they back off on their own. This isn't "theory" or imagination; I've observed this both times in the recent events and many times amongst dogs outside of my pack. It also doesn't mean you won't need to correct the "assisting pack"; in fact, unless they are balanced, you must COUNT on correcting them all the while handling the initial problem. Then, back to everyone calming down and ending the event by them being together.

While I was been writing this outside on the lanai, all of the dogs were napping, wandering the yard, and generally just being dogs. That's Koa's nature, it's what Faith needs, and Piper is learning that it's okay for dogs to like her and want to be around her. Faith invited Piper to play shortly after the explosion, so all is well in the doggie mind world.

Until next time, stay calm and unaffected by stress!

Transformation in Dogs and Humans

Sunday was a sad and joyful day all at once… Faith returned to her home after being with us and having 9 days of intense rehabilitation. She got a chance to hang out with an extremely balanced group of people and pack of dogs. Faith went from being very withdrawn and one-dimensional in the social dog world to opening up and enjoying being around the crowd.

None of Faith's problems had anything to do with Stewart & Arlene, her owners. They are 1000% committed to doing whatever it takes to have Faith learn to live in their pack, and expand her possibilities as a dog. Because of her issues, they could have just as easily – after 3 weeks – given her back up because she is too much work and "a dangerous dog". For that, and the fact that they picked me to help them with that, I am extremely honored and incredibly grateful. Faith taught and challenged me, she taught the pack, and more importantly the pack taught her that while she bit every one of them in the beginning (mostly all in one morning walk) it didn't mean that they held a grudge against her. Even our cat doesn't hold a grudge simply because Faith initially got her mouth around him to bite him before I stopped it. Now, they get along as if they've always lived alongside each other.

It's said that the pack teaches faster than the human can and I've seen that in action many times, but with Faith the

pack – by its Exclusion of her rather than its Inclusion – taught her that the fun starts with being balanced. It never happened again after Faith's owners went on vacation and Faith stayed at Kamp K-9 Jax Bch for a week and a half. She had rituals – not "I'll show you" type of exercises, but those designed to bring out the dog in her – every day. And even when I had another dog along with Koa, within one day Faith began inviting the dogs to play with an intensity I have never seen before... as if to say, "I have 9 years to make up for; let's get started NOW!" It was hilarious!

This morning on the pack walk Arlene and Faith walked with us, not separate but WITH us. This was as much for

Arlene as it was for Faith to be back with the pack. Faith sniffed, explored with the boys (Koa, MC and Atticus), she inserted herself and walked along with the human pack, and even started to try to get into the wrestling match between Koa and MC to rough play with them. Incredible

transformation in a short period! Of course, the humans are the ones unsure about a response because we live in the past whereas dogs live in the present. I'm looking forward to the day where Faith – at 9 years old – gives the whippersnappers a run for their money in the rough housing department! And that will be sooner rather than later...

So what do we take away from this? Being calm, patient, living in the present, seeing what you want rather than what has happened, and allowing yourself to trust the dog (and, in turn, showing the dog that the pack leader expects trustworthy states of mind), are the keys to the doors we have yet to open with our dogs. Even balanced dogs (and sometimes Pack Leaders) need direction and reminders of limitations, but humans can't look at that as a failure on the part of the dog. It is no failure at all; that is the lifelong responsibility you take on when you decide to own a dog and assimilate them into your family.

Look at your dog right now... go on, do it. Go into the other room, or turn around in your chair as I am doing to look at your pack member resting comfortably, playing, or eating or whatever, and think: Is this little/big creature a joy or a chore? Do they make my life better or worse? How much better/worse would my life be if they suddenly were gone? Look for the positive, joyful things your dog brings to your life and remember that when they

misbehave. That only means that really need YOU!

Until the next time, stay calm and enjoy the dogs in your life!

Kamp K-9 Jax Bch LIVE in local NBC Studio!

G reg and The Pack travelled to the local NBC studios for a segment during First Coast Living! The Pack consisted of Koa (of course), Faith, and Redford (two long-term boarders with me right now). Through my expertise on the law enforcement security and safety side, I have been interviewed often over the years so I knew what to expect. What I was curious to find out is how the dogs would do in a very different environment (lights, movement, people, shiny/slick floors, etc.). I was certain about Koa, since he buddies up with me almost everywhere I go.

When we arrived in the lobby, all of the dogs were careful and respectful. After signing waivers and such the other guests and we were escorted in the direction of the studio. When I say escorted, the producer held the door and while the other guests waited and we kept walking straight past them. Koa seemed to know his way: past the news desk cubicle area, left into a multiple studio area, right into the ante area of that day's studio and left into the waiting area on the set (maybe I should Google Koa's name to see what he's been doing at NBC late at night…).

Amazingly, Redford and Faith were completely calm (as in they sacked out on the carpet) while Koa was taking in all the sights and seemed at home (once again, this concerns me). Lisa was able to come and watched over the pack while I went over graphics and correct spellings with the producer. Everyone was very congenial and respectful to the dogs and they were respectful in return. Co-host Curtis Dvorak (who, for 19 years, was an amazing Jaxon DeVille (mascot) for the Jacksonville Jaguars) stopped by

to chat and mugged with the dogs, trying to get Redford to kiss him while Koa stretched out on his other side.

I mentioned shiny floors in studios before, and that was on my mind because that is Koa's kryptonite (besides thunder); he has always been a little iffy on floors that are slick. Between the waiting areas and the sets are slick floors where the cameras and the production staff move around. Since after the opening remarks and the weather it would be our turn, when the producer told us to take our place in the "living room" area of the set, I got up and walked forward with a purpose – since we only had one minute. Koa and the pack moved right along and although Koa seemed to be picking his steps, he plowed ahead and took his place, stretched out on the rug in front of the couch, much like he does every night on a different rug. Redford and Faith sat calmly while the producer was adjusting the microphone and make-up, and then the countdown began.

If you have watched the segment, Faith decided that once the photos started rolling on the monitor behind us, that she would fixate on the one that shows me walking the five dogs. If fact, she looked like she was looking out a window

and wondering why everyone was walking without her, while showing her butt to the camera the whole time. What you COULDN'T see, once the end of the interview came and they cut away to the graphics, Faith decided to explore behind the monitor to see what was behind "the window". Clearly finding nothing, she came back to the set and sat down for some pictures. She's no dummy...

Leaving the set, the dogs had no problem following calmly (even Koa over the shiny floors again) and we turned over the mike and started out. This time we were not escorted and once again the dogs, without pulling but clearly showing me the correct way back out and in reverse without a misstep, lead me out of the maze of a building. In fact, at one point while I stopped to consider my options for the way out, Koa essentially displayed the "follow me" attitude... and he was right! Once out the door we ran to the car for treats, and the rest of the whole day was a nap-fest for all of them.

This was actually not a journal for the appearance, but a teaching point inside of a story. Being a Pack Leader is more about listening than it is telling. Yes, we have to direct our packs but often leaders who don't listen to their

packs don't get a clear picture of their packs' direction. Pack leaders don't know everything but they ARE in charge of everything. Trust in the dog is a major component of leadership, and trusting that Koa would be okay with the shiny floors and not babying him is better leadership than many alternatives. The dogs also knew the way into and out of the studio... how? And why? I don't know the answer to that, but I followed at the right time and then went back to leading at the appropriate time. They led at the right time, and they went back to following at the right time. That's not just leadership in action, that's teamwork in action. Many human teams wish that they could work so well and so seamlessly than that... I've been on some of those kinds of teams that don't do well.

Until the next time, stay calm and trustworthy to become the leader your pack needs!

Thank you, Faith!

Today is a mixed emotion day: Faith, the 11-year-old Airedale and my long-term buddy, had to be put to rest due to quickly diminishing health. It's a mixed emotion because, first of all, it is extremely sad to lose a dog and I feel terrible for Arlene & Stewart, Faith's tremendously committed pack leaders. It's an extremely hard decision to make and one that came after long discussions and thoughts on how to best honor Faith. In the end, we have to do what is best for our companions and this is the best decision possible – we all don't want Faith suffering and/or embarrassed or scared by her health issues at the end of her life.

At the other end of the emotional/human side is the celebration of a life that had an extremely bad start for 9 years, then was rescued and fostered by some folks and eventually adopted by Arlene & Stewart who gave her a life better than even her foster family. I met Faith through a contact because Faith had fairly significant dog aggression issues (for the full story read, "Having Faith in Faith") so rather than rewrite that chapter, I want to tell you about some of her escapades.

Lisa had a ton of old videos on her phone of Faith playing with a friend's puppy with 2 other dogs. Faith taught me a valuable lesson about dog aggression and where it comes from. In her particular case, it came from being the puppy mill mom she was for 9 years – only crated, never really out around other dogs except to mate, and always correcting and directing puppies. Her dog socialization was strictly about keeping the peace all of the time, and lots of rules/boundaries/limitations. If anyone else gets too close canine moms will become very fierce and will protect at all costs. But they are also fierce pack leaders with their own pack.

Faith was still an anomaly because she would correct small & young dogs with the same ferociousness as adult dogs…

but not always. As an Airedale, she "soft mouths" dogs but very quickly and suddenly with a certainty that she meant business. Faith would also welcome dogs at Kamp K-9 Jax Bch with extreme interest but in a way more playful mode than originally demonstrated with the beach pack (she bit 5 of 6 dogs in the first hour, including Koa from behind!). However, I still used Faith a number of times to play with younger dogs because she knew how to manage their energy better than any human could in a balanced way. I wanted her to pay it forward, and she never disappointed.

As you might remember, I had Faith with me during our television appearance that included Koa and Redford. Faith actually stole the show in the studio: she napped while we all did a meet and greet with the on-air talent but when she came on the set in front of the camera she kept watching the big monitor right behind us. When they put up a picture of me walking a large pack she apparently wanted to go, too. As they broke for additional information Faith wandered off the set and behind the monitor to see where the pack was and when I called her back she returned to the set just in time for the camera to return to us. Yet all you could see was her butt because she kept staring at the screen, a.k.a. "looking out the window".

If you have ever been on the set of a live TV show, there

are a lot of distractions and things have to run rather quickly. It's a lot for humans to process if you are not used to it, but a huge job for dogs. Everyone at the station and behind the scenes enjoyed having them around. Since I knew that all 3 of these guys were going to do well and I wanted a cross section of ages so that people could see that old & young dogs can be calm. In my mind, Faith stole the show with displaying her intense interest in wanting to walk with the pack and acting younger than the young boys.

We got to see Faith one last time the night before she went running across the Rainbow Bridge into the waiting excitement of fields dogs that have gone before her (don't correct the little ones, Faith!). She was excited to see Lisa and I but you could tell she was not feeling the way she wanted to feel. Her hugs were the same, she leaned her head against us the same, but obviously, she was tired. She even struggled to her feet on her own to walk us out as we left. As sad as that can be, we saved the sadness until we left because with her we celebrated a life well displayed and recounted the things that made us rejoice in her life with all of us. How could you not?

So, thank you, Faith, for teaching me new things about dog psychology and instinct. Thank you for helping me pass this information along to other dog owners. Thank you for showing me that doing the right thing with your dog will give you the desired results. Thank you for the snuggles and the hugs. Thank you for loving all of the humans you ever came into contact with because we all loved you very much. Thank you for your searching eyes looking for approval when you wanted to know if what you were doing was okay. Thank you for listening when we said it wasn't okay.

The biggest THANK YOU with an outpouring of love and respect goes to Arlene & Stewart for staying CONSISTENT in their goals, their work and their unwavering love for a dog that had a hugely bad start. But because of her last 2 years with them she had the life she deserved with owners whose flood of love and commitment is what we all strive to do with our dogs. I have been honored to have worked with you guys and honored to work with Faith, but I'm most honored and humbled by your commitment and dedication to helping Faith in her life with you.

Rest in peace, my curly friend; we will all see each other again one day... And for everyone else, stay consistent with your goals and be Pack Leaders like Arlene & Stewart.

About The Author

Greg DiFranza, also known as the "Pack Leader", is a retired sheriff's deputy with the Jacksonville (FL) Sheriff's Office where he served as a training coordinator for Field Force, Dive Team, and was assigned to the Police Academy as an officer survival instructor. Following his career he started WinFirst International, Inc. where he also taught globally for 30 years with the Institute of Police Technology and Management as their Tactical Unit Coordinator, teaching officer survival and narcotics enforcement.

He also owns and operates First Coast Kodokan Judo, where he is a Yodan (4th degree black belt) and still competes internationally. A 5-time National Heavyweight Champion, and 7-time World Heavyweight Champion, he was recently named USA Judo Top Ranked Master's Athlete in the 60 year old division.

He and his wife Lisa live in Jacksonville, FL with their Rhodesian Ridgeback, Koa, and their Blue Tabby Birman cat, Shaka, where they all enjoy outside activities…

And dogs.